CW01594555

TWENTY-SIX MEN AND A GIRL

AND OTHER STORIES

BY

MAXIM GORKY

TRANSLATED FROM THE RUSSIAN BY

EMILY JAKOWLEFF & DORA B. MONTEFIORE

WITH AN INTRODUCTION BY

EDWARD GARNETT

NEW YORK

FREDERICK A. STOKES COMPANY

1915

In the interest of creating a more extensive selection of rare historical book reprints, we have chosen to reproduce this title even though it may possibly have occasional imperfections such as missing and blurred pages, missing text, poor pictures, markings, dark backgrounds and other reproduction issues beyond our control. Because this work is culturally important, we have made it available as a part of our commitment to protecting, preserving and promoting the world's literature. Thank you for your understanding.

Undergraduate Library
Transfer to Storage 11 7-87
1689
11-14-38
37319

CONTENTS

* *Note.—The translation of Tchelkash is the work of S. K. Michel.*

MAXIM GORKY.

It is always instructive to watch the public's reception of new writers. So little depends, comparatively speaking, on a writer's merits, and so much depends as to whether the public feel sympathy with his picture of life, and can reconcile it with the particular atmosphere and ethical outlook of its own world. Thus, the public often sees an artistic excellence which does not exist in the writers whose work fortifies society in its passing point of view and dresses out prevalent ideas in an approving garb. Artistically, their work may be contemptible, but how uncommonly acute and gifted do those writers appear to society who justify its preconceptions! Herein lies the popularity of those swarms of mediocre works that each year are stacked before us—only to be thrown on to the dust heaps of the year after. Such works have but reflected, without beauty, the common thought, the very common tendency of the moment; they quickly grow limp, and cannot be resuscitated.

When writers of real power appear, their popularity is also a question as to whether society can *utilize* their vision of life, and make it serve people's immediate needs; and such artists often attract an attention disproportionate to their actual merits. Thus, Tennyson's work was seized on by the nation when Browning's and Meredith's contemporary writings were welcomed by a few hundred people. The case of Maxim Gorky in Russia to-day is a good example of the sudden rage that may attack a public for a man's writings. Gorky has been writing since 1894, but he has to-day become the fashion: the greatest things are expected of his talent, and the result of a recent Government *surveillance* of the author is to double his popularity, and place him, as an artist, in rather a false position. The Russian public, in fact, is trying to *utilise* Gorky's pictures of life, and make them serve a special end.

There are, however, some good reasons why the Russian public should be devoting itself to Gorky to-day. In the first place, he has a really original talent which is seen to advantage in the comparative dearth of new Russian novelists; and in the second place, the tone of his work is unusually strong, healthy, and independent, while his analysis of life is as uncompromising as the Russian mind demands. Gorky, who has come into literature out of the ranks of the manual labourers and the tramps, brings into the bored atmosphere of the cultured class something of the vigour and directness which belong to the outcasts who live from day to day by their wits, and are always face to face with the harshest realities. To this directness and vigour of tone, Gorky joins a delicacy of poetic feeling which has enabled him to give very profound studies of the Russian character—as in Ignát and Mayakin in his novel *Fomá Gordyéeff*, and in his story *Konovalov*. It is natural, therefore, that the Russian public should now look to Gorky, next to Tolstoy, to express that general *malaise* of soul, that discontent with the conditions of life which is more or less chronic in Russia. In Gorky's sketches the public find also the feeling for common humanity, a sympathy with the most degraded outcasts, a bitter appreciation of life's brutalities, and a discontent with all slavishness, expressed in a manner so fresh and vigorous that Russians are not unnaturally looking to the author to give people the lead in a political direction—a new direction which nobody can exactly define.

We, in England, however, are simply concerned with Gorky, the artist, and it is to be hoped that though his work may not fortify us exactly in our practice, let alone in our prejudice, Gorky's true spirituality may not be misapprehended among us.

Differences in the interpretation of an artist's spirit arise from the different standpoints of the spectators, and it is a fact that many English popular idealistic writers, to Russian eyes, seem either hopelessly childish or hopelessly immoral. There is, in fact, this natural difference between the two attitudes to life. The English-speaking world honestly favours those writers whose pictures show the ultimate triumph of the moral law over life's ugliness and nature's indifference. If a writer shows men's animal natures getting the better of their instincts towards fineness, while life is not painted "as it ought to be," and beauty made synonymous with "moral effort," we complain of him as a "depressing" and "unpleasant" writer. Perhaps we do not deny the writer's truth, but the critics are apt to label him "powerful but repulsive." The Russian-speaking world, on the other hand, is quite intolerant of cheap idealism, and finds its satisfaction largely in those analyses of men's motives, good and bad, which show the insufficiency of "the moral law" to dictate to nature and dominate it; the difference being that, to the Russian mind, it is immoral to conceal or falsify the seamy facts in a world so constantly dominated by ugliness, while, to the English mind, it is immoral not to let fine character and conscience have the final word "in the battle of life." The admirable story here printed of "Twenty-six and One" is, however, a good illustration of the fact that the art that analyses human nature is immeasurably superior to the art which falsifies human nature to suit a moral purpose—the simple spirit of love by which the girl Tanya brings precious things into the dreary life of the twenty-six men being the same love which she bestows on her seducer, by which she is justified in the moment of trial.

It is too much to expect that Gorky will be popular in England, but still his work may be of some service. He can be of use at least in the sense that every honest analysis of life, artistically put, is a natural corrective of those melodramatic, pretentious, pseudo presentations which our "popular" fiction and our popular stage supply *ad libitum* to the undiscerning crowd. Gorky's work is the natural antidote to novels of the inflated type, which are daily hailed as "masterpieces," to novels of life *de luxe* for the Pulman car. We have no wish to single out any work in particular from scores of "fictions" that are alike false to life and false to art. We merely cite the last fashionable fiction as it serves as a good example of those gorgeously-upholstered "works of art," in which the hero's emotions are laid less open to us than is the heroine's *lingerie*; those "architectured" novels in which the vast historic Manor House, and the "deer park," the racing stables, the sumptuously-fitted yacht, and the Riviera chateau, the abnormal hero driving his four-in-hand, and the voluptuous "enchantress," in her "delicate transparent night-dress," in her "sea green dressing-gown," form the ravishing motive, and make indeed a truthful analysis of life almost wholly superfluous, if not impossible. In Gorky we find no circulating library "aristocratic" emotions to admire, and no up-to-date Puritanic eroticism to smile at. A superabundance of costly surroundings, together with an extremely falsified psychological analysis, the English public has had a weakness for in its fiction since the days of Bulwer Lytton. But we will not pursue the embarrassing comparison further; it is sufficient to say that Gorky offers us no wicked Neapolitan *mise-en-scène*, no stage-managed plots. He has sinned slightly in one or two romantic tales, such as *Makar Chudra*, but only slightly. It is difficult to sum up Gorky as an artist. It is difficult for the reason that so many of Gorky's tales are merely bits of narrative, slices of life represented much as they happened. Such narratives show insight, vigour, and truth to life; but the artist is not in sufficient evidence in the composition or selection of the material. Thus, in *My Fellow-Traveller*, Shakro is a most convincing study of a man; but the story is not fine as a work of art—it is an interesting slice out of life. We should have inferred, therefore, that Gorky's absorption in life tended to get the better of his instincts as an artist were it not for the evidence of such stories as *On a Raft*. This latter story is a very fine psychological analysis, by which the reader penetrates into the minds of the four characters in turn, rapidly shifts his own moral judgment, and is left to murmur the lines:—

> "Before ye gie poor frailty names,
> Suppose a change o' cases."

Occasionally Gorky rises to a high level of excellence. One or two of his chapters, indeed (such as Chapter XI.), in *Foma Gordyéeff*,* show such remarkable appreciation of character, that it is clear Gorky's talent is worth watching. The four stories here presented to the English reader are typical examples of Gorky's art.

EDWARD GARNETT.

* *Foma Gordyéeff.* By Maxim Gorky. Translated by Isabel F. Hapgood. (London: T. Fisher Unwin.)

TWENTY-SIX MEN AND A GIRL.

There were six-and-twenty of us;—six-and-twenty living machines in a damp, underground cellar, where from morning till night we kneaded dough and rolled it into kringels. Opposite the underground window of our cellar was a bricked area, green and mouldy with moisture. The window was protected from outside with a close iron grating, and the light of the sun could not pierce through the window panes, covered as they were with flour dust.

Our employer had bars placed in front of the windows, so that we should not be able to give a bit of his bread to passing beggars, or to any of our fellows who were out of work and hungry. Our employer called us rogues, and gave us half-rotten tripe to eat for our mid-day meal, instead of meat. It was swelteringly close for us cooped up in that stone underground chamber, under the low, heavy, soot-blackened, cobwebby ceiling. Dreary and sickening was our life between its thick, dirty, mouldy walls.

Unrefreshed, and with a feeling of not having had our sleep out, we used to get up at five o'clock in the morning; and before six, we were already seated, worn out and apathetic, at the table, rolling out the dough which our mates had already prepared whilst we slept. The whole day, from ten in the early morning until ten at night, some of us sat round that table, working up in our hands the yielding paste, rolling it to and fro so that it should not get stiff; whilst the others kneaded the swelling mass of dough. And the whole day the simmering water in the kettle, where the kringels were being cooked, sang low and sadly; and the baker's shovel scraped harshly over the oven floor, as he threw the slippery bits of dough out of the kettle on to the heated bricks.

From morning till evening wood was burning in the oven, and the red glow of the fire gleamed and flickered over the walls of the bake-shop, as if silently mocking us. The giant oven was like the misshapen head of a monster in a fairy tale; it thrust itself up out of the floor, opened wide jaws, full of glowing fire, and blew hot breath upon us; it seemed to be ever watching out of its black air-holes our interminable work. Those two deep holes were like eyes—the cold, pitiless eyes of a monster. They watched us always with the same darkened glance, as if they were weary of seeing before them such eternal slaves, from whom they could expect nothing human, and therefore scorned them with the cold scorn of wisdom.

In meal dust, in the mud which we brought in from the yard on our boots, in the hot, sticky atmosphere, day in, day out, we rolled the dough into kringels, which we moistened with our own sweat. And we hated our work with a glowing hatred; we never ate what had passed through our hands, and preferred black bread to kringels. Sitting opposite each other, at a long table—nine facing nine—we moved our hands and fingers mechanically during endlessly long hours, till we were so accustomed to our monotonous work that we ceased to pay any attention to it.

We had all studied each other so constantly, that each of us knew every wrinkle of his mates' faces. It was not long also before we had exhausted almost every topic of conversation; that is why we were most of the time silent, unless we were chaffing each other; but one cannot always find something about which to chaff another man, especially when that man is one's mate. Neither were we much given to finding fault with one another; how, indeed, could one of us poor devils be in a position to find fault with another, when we were all of us half dead and, as it were, turned to stone? For the heavy drudgery seemed to crush all feeling out of us. But silence is only terrible and fearful for those who have said everything and have nothing more to say to each other; for men, on the contrary, who have never begun to communicate with one another, it is easy and simple.

Sometimes, too, we sang; and this is how it happened that we began to sing: one of us would sigh deeply in the midst of our toil, like an overdriven horse, and then we would begin one of those songs whose gentle swaying melody seems always to ease the burden on the singer's heart.

At first one sang by himself, and we others sat in silence listening to his solitary song, which, under the heavy vaulted roof of the cellar, died gradually away, and became extinguished, like a little fire in the steppes, on a wet autumn night, when the grey heaven hangs like a heavy mass over the earth. Then another would join in with the singer, and now two soft, sad voices would break into song in our narrow, dull hole of a cellar. Suddenly others would join in, and the song would roll forward like a wave, would grow louder and swell upwards, till it would seem as if the damp, foul walls of our stone prison were widening out and opening. Then, all six-and-twenty of us would be singing; our loud, harmonious song would fill the whole cellar, our voices would travel outside and beyond, striking, as it were, against the walls in moaning sobs and sighs, moving our hearts with soft, tantalizing ache, tearing open old wounds, and awakening longings.

The singers would sigh deeply and heavily; suddenly one would become silent and listen to the others singing, then let his voice flow once more in the common tide. Another would exclaim in a stifled voice, "Ah!" and would shut his eyes, whilst the deep, full sound waves would show him, as it were, a road, in front of him—a sunlit, broad road in the distance, which he himself, in thought, wandered along.

But the flame flickers once more in the huge oven, the baker scrapes incessantly with his shovel, the water simmers in the kettle, and the flicker of the fire on the wall dances as before in silent mockery. While in other men's words we sing out our dumb grief, the weary burden of live men robbed of the sunlight, the burden of slaves.

So we lived, we six-and-twenty, in the vault-like cellar of a great stone house, and we suffered each one of us, as if we had to bear on our shoulders the whole three storeys of that house.

But we had something else good, besides the singing—something we loved, that perhaps took the place of the sunshine.

In the second storey of our house there was established a gold-embroiderer's shop, and there, living amongst the other embroidery girls, was Tanya, a little maid-servant of sixteen. Every morning there peeped in through the glass door a rosy little face, with merry blue eyes; while a ringing, tender voice called out to us:

"Little prisoners! Have you any kringels, please, for me?"

At that clear sound, we knew so well, we all used to turn round, gazing with simple-hearted joy at the pure girlish face which smiled at us so sweetly. The sight of the small nose pressed against the window-pane, and of the white teeth gleaming between the half-open lips, had become for us a daily pleasure. Tumbling over each other we used to jump up to open the door, and she would step in, bright and cheerful, holding out her apron, with her head thrown on one side, and a smile on her lips. Her thick, long chesnut hair fell over her shoulder and across her breast. But we, ugly, dirty and misshapen as we were, looked up at her—the threshold door was four steps above the floor—looked up at her with heads thrown back, wishing her good morning, and speaking strange unaccustomed words, which we kept for her only. Our voices became softer when we spoke to her, our jests were lighter. For her—everything was different with us. The baker took from his oven a shovel of the best and the brownest kringels, and threw them deftly into Tanya's apron.

"Be off with you now, or the boss will catch you!" we warned her each time. She laughed roguishly, called out cheerfully: "Good bye, poor prisoners!" and slipped away as quick as a mouse.

That was all. But long after she had gone

we talked about her to one another with pleasure. It was always the same thing as we had said yesterday and the day before, because everything about us, including ourselves and her, remained the same—as yesterday—and as always.

Painful and terrible it is when a man goes on living, while nothing changes around him; and when such an existence does not finally kill his soul, then the monotony becomes with time, even more and more painful. Generally we spoke about women in such a way, that sometimes it was loathsome to us ourselves to hear our rude, shameless talk. The women whom we knew deserved perhaps nothing better. But about Tanya we never let fall an evil word; none of us ever ventured so much as to lay a hand on her, even too free a jest she never heard from us. Maybe this was so because she never remained for long with us; she flashed on our eyes like a star falling from the sky, and vanished; and maybe because she was little and very beautiful, and everything beautiful calls forth respect, even in coarse people. And besides—though our life of penal labour had made us dull beasts, oxen, we were still men, and, like all men, could not live without worshipping something or other. Better than her we had none, and none but she took any notice of us, living in the cellar—no one, though there were dozens of people in the house. And then, too—most likely, this was the chief thing—we all regarded her as something of our own, something existing as it were only by virtue of our kringels. We took on ourselves in turns the duty of providing her with hot kringels, and this became for us like a daily sacrifice to our idol, it became almost a sacred rite, and every day it bound us more closely to her. Besides kringels, we gave Tanya a great deal of advice—to wear warmer clothes, not to run upstairs too quickly, not to carry heavy bundles of wood. She listened to all our counsels with a smile, answered them by a laugh, and never took our advice, but we were not offended at that; all we wanted was to show how much care we bestowed upon her.

Often she would apply to us with different requests, she asked us for instance to open the heavy door into the store-cellar, and to chop wood: with delight and a sort of pride, we did this for her and everything else she wanted.

But when one of us asked her to mend his solitary shirt for him, she said, with a laugh of contempt:

"What next! A likely idea!"

We made great fun of the queer fellow who could entertain such an idea, and—never asked her to do anything else. We loved her—all is said in that. Man always wants to lay his love on someone, though sometimes he crushes, sometimes he sullies, with it; he may poison another life because he loves without respecting the beloved. We were bound to love Tanya, for we had no one else to love.

At times one of us would suddenly begin to reason like this:

"And why do we make so much of the wench? What is there in her? eh? What a to-do we make about her!"

The man who dared to utter such words we promptly and coarsely cut short—we wanted something to love: we had found it and loved it, and what we twenty-six loved must be for each of us unalterable, as a holy thing, and anyone who acted against us in this was our enemy. We loved, maybe, not what was really good, but you see there were twenty-six of us, and so we always wanted to see what was precious to us held sacred by the rest.

Our love is not less burdensome than hate, and maybe that is just why some proud souls maintain that our hate is more flattering than our love. But why do they not run away from us, if it is so?

. . . .

Besides our department our employer had also a bread-bakery; it was in the same house, separated from our hole only by a wall; but the bakers—there were four of them—held aloof from us, considering their work superior to ours, and therefore themselves better than us; they never used to come into our workroom, and laughed contemptuously at us when they met us in the yard. We, too, did not go to see them; this was forbidden by our employer, from fear that we should steal the fancy bread. We did not like the bakers, because we envied them; their work was lighter than ours, they were paid more, and were better fed; they had a light, spacious workroom, and they were all so clean and healthy—and that make them hateful to us. We all looked grey and yellow; three of us had syphilis, several suffered from skin diseases, one was completely crippled by rheumatism. On holidays and in their leisure time the bakers wore pea-jackets and creaking boots, two of them had accordions, and they all used to go for strolls in the town gardens,—we wore filthy rags and leather clogs or plaited shoes on our feet, the police would not let us into the town gardens—could we possibly like the bakers?

And one day we learned that their chief baker had been drunk, the master had sacked him and had already taken on another, and that this other was a soldier, wore a satin waistcoat and a watch and gold chain. We were inquisitive to get a sight of such a dandy, and in the hope of catching a glimpse of him we kept running one after another out into the yard.

But he came of his own accord into our room. Kicking at the door, he pushed it open, and leaving it ajar, stood in the doorway smiling, and said to us:

"God help the work! Good morning, mates!"

The ice-cold air, which streamed in through the open door, curled in streaks of vapour round his feet. He stood on the threshold, looked us up and down, and under his fair, twisted moustache gleamed big yellow teeth. His waistcoat was really something quite out of the common, blue-flowered, brilliant with shining little buttons of red stones. He also wore a watch chain.

He was a fine fellow, this soldier; tall, healthy, rosy-cheeked, and his big, clear eyes had a friendly, cheerful glance. He wore on his head a white starched cap, and from under his spotlessly clean apron peeped the pointed toes of fashionable, well-blacked boots.

Our baker asked him politely to shut the door. The soldier did so without hurrying himself, and began to question us about the master. We explained to him, all speaking together, that our employer was a thorough-going brute, a rogue, a knave, and a slave-driver; in a word we repeated to him all that can and must be said about an employer, but cannot be repeated here. The soldier listened to us, twisted his moustache, and watched us with a friendly, openhearted look.

"But haven't you got a lot of girls here?" he asked, suddenly.

Some of us began to laugh deferentially, others put on a meaning expression, and one of us explained to the soldier that there were nine girls here.

"You make the most of them?" asked the soldier, with a wink.

We laughed, but not so loudly, and with some embarassment. Many of us would have liked to have shown the soldier that we also were tremendous fellows with the girls, but not one of us could do so; and one of our number confessed as much, when he said in a low voice:

"That sort of thing is not in our line."

"Well no, it wouldn't quite do for you," said the soldier with conviction, after having looked us over. "There is something wanting about you all. You don't look the right sort. You've no sort of appearance; and the women, you see, they like a bold appearance, they will have a well set up body. Everything has to be tip-top for them. That's why they respect strength. They want an arm like that!"

The soldier drew his right hand, with its turned-up shirt sleeve, out of his pocket, and showed us his bare arm. It was white and strong, and covered with shining yellow hairs.

"Leg and chest, all must be strong. And then a man must be dressed in the latest fashion, so as to show off his looks to advantage. Yes, all the women take to me. Whether I call to them, or whether I beckon them, they with one accord, five at a time, throw themselves at my head."

He sat down on a flour sack, and told at length all about the way women loved him, and how bold he was with them. Then he left, and after the door had creaked to behind him, we sat for a long time silent, and thought about him and his talk. Then we all suddenly broke silence together, and it became apparent that we were all equally pleased with him. He was such a nice, open-hearted fellow; he came to see us without any stand-offishness, sat down and chatted. No one else came to us like that, and no one else talked to us in that friendly sort of way. And we continued to talk of him and his coming triumph among the embroidery girls, who passed us by with contemptuous sniffs when they saw us in the yard, or who looked straight through us as if we had been air. But we admired them always when we met them outside, or when they walked past our windows; in winter, in fur jackets and toques to match; in summer, in hats trimmed with flowers, and with coloured parasols in their hands. We talked, however, about these girls in a way that would have made them mad with shame and rage, if they could have heard us.

"If only he does not get hold of little Tanya!" said the baker, suddenly, in an anxious tone of voice.

We were silent, for these words troubled us. Tanya had quite gone out of our minds, supplanted, put on one side by the strong, fine figure of the soldier.

Then began a lively discussion; some of us maintained that Tanya would never lower herself so; others thought she would not be able to resist him, and the third group proposed to give him a thrashing if he should try to annoy Tanya. And, finally, we all decided to watch the soldier and Tanya, and to warn the girl against him. This brought the discussion to an end.

Four weeks had passed by since then; during this time the soldier baked white bread, walked about with the gold-embroidery girls, visited us often, but did not talk any more about his conquests; only twisted his moustache, and licked his lips lasciviously.

Tanya called in as usual every morning for "little kringels," and was as gay and as nice and friendly with us as ever. We certainly tried once or twice to talk to her about the soldier, but she called him a "goggle-eyed calf," and made fun of him all round, and that set our minds at rest. We saw how the gold-embroidery girls carried on with the soldier, and we were proud of our girl; Tanya's behaviour reflected honour on us all; we imitated her, and began in our talks to treat the soldier with small consideration. She became dearer to us, and we greeted her with more friendliness and kindliness every morning.

One day the soldier came to see us, a bit drunk, and sat down and began to laugh. When we asked him what he was laughing about, he explained to us:

"Why two of them—that Lydka girl and Grushka—have been clawing each other on my account. You should have seen the way they went for each other! Ha! ha! One got hold of the other one by the hair, threw her down on the floor of the passage, and sat on her! Ha! ha! ha! They scratched and tore each others' faces. It was enough to make one die with laughter! Why is it women can't fight fair? Why do they always scratch one another, eh?"

He sat on the bench, healthy, fresh and jolly

he sat there and went on laughing. We were silent. This time he made an unpleasant impression on us.

"Well, its a funny thing what luck I have with the women-folk! Eh? I've laughed till I'm ill! One wink, and it's all over with them! Its the d-devil!"

He raised his white hairy hands, and slapped them down on his knees. And his eyes seem to reflect such frank astonishment, as if he were himself quite surprised at his good luck with women. His fat red face glistened with delight and self satisfaction, and he licked his lips more than ever.

Our baker scraped the shovel violently and angrily along the oven floor, and all at once he said sarcastically:

"There's no great strength needed to pull up fir saplings, but try a real pine-tree."

"Why—what do you mean by saying that to me? asked the soldier.

"Oh, well . . ."

"What is it?"

"Nothing—it slipped out!"

"No, wait a minute! What's the point? What pine-tree?"

Our baker did not answer, working rapidly away with the shovel at the oven; flinging into it the half-cooked kringels, taking out those that were done, and noisily throwing them on the floor to the boys who were stringing them on bast. He seemed to have forgotten the soldier and his conversation with him. But the soldier had all at once dropped into a sort of uneasiness. He got up on to his feet, and went to the oven, at the risk of knocking against the handle of the shovel, which was waving spasmodically in the air.

"No, tell me, do—who is it? You've insulted me. I? There's not one could withstand me, n-no! And you say such insulting things to me?"

He really seemed genuinely hurt. He must have had nothing else to pride himself on except his gift for seducing women; maybe, except for that, there was nothing living in him, and it was only that by which he could feel himself a living man.

There are men to whom the most precious and best thing in their lives appears to be some disease of their soul or body. They spend their whole life in relation to it, and only living by it, suffering from it, they sustain themselves on it, they complain of it to others, and so draw the attention of their fellows to themselves. For that they extract sympathy from people, and apart from it they have nothing at all. Take from them that disease, cure them, and they will be miserable, because they have lost their one resource in life—they are left empty then. Sometimes a man's life is so poor, that he is driven instinctively to prize his vice and to live by it; one may say for a fact that often men are vicious from boredom.

The soldier was offended, he went up to our baker and roared:

"No, tell me do—who?"

"Tell you?" the baker turned suddenly to him.

"Well?"

"You know Tanya?"

"Well?"

"Well, there then! Only try."

"I?"

"You!"

"Her? Why that's nothing to me—pooh!"

"We shall see!'

"You will see! Ha! ha!"

"She'll——"

"Give me a month!"

"What a braggart you are, soldier! '

"A fortnight! I'll prove it! Who is it? Tanya! Pooh!"

"Well, get out. You're in my way!"

"A fortnight—and it's done! Ah, you——"

"Get out, I say!"

Our baker, all at once, flew into a rage and brandished his shovel. The soldier staggered away from him in amazement, looked at us, paused, and softly, malignantly said, "Oh, all right, then!" and went away.

During the dispute we had all sat silent, absorbed in it. But when the soldier had gone, eager, loud talk and noise arose among us.

Some one shouted to the baker: "It's a bad job that you've started, Pavel!"

"Do your work!" answered the baker, savagely.

We felt that the soldier had been deeply aggrieved, and that danger threatened Tanya. We felt this, and at the same time we were all possessed by a burning curiosity, most agreeable to us. What would happen? Would Tanya hold out against the soldier? And almost all cried confidently: "Tanya? She'll hold out! You won't catch her with your bare arms!"

We longed terribly to test the strength of our idol; we forcibly proved to each other that our divinity was a strong divinity and would come victorious out of this ordeal. We began at last to fancy that we had not worked enough on the soldier, that he would forget the dispute, and that we ought to pique his vanity more keenly. From that day we began to live a different life, a life of nervous tension, such as we had never known before. We spent whole days in arguing together; we all grew, as it were, sharper; and got to talk more and better. It seemed to us that we were playing some sort of game with the devil, and the stake on our side was Tanya. And when we learnt from the bakers that the soldier had begun "running after our Tanya," we felt a sort of delighted terror, and life was so interesting that we did not even notice that our employer had taken advantage of our pre-occupation to increase our work by fourteen pounds of dough a day. We seemed, indeed, not even tired by our work. Tanya's name was on our lips all day long. And every day we looked for her with a certain special impatience. Sometimes we pictured to ourselves that she would come to us, and it would not be the same Tanya as of old, but somehow different. We said nothing to her, however, of the dispute regarding her. We asked her no questions, and behaved as well and affectionately to her as ever. But even in this a new element crept in, alien to our old feeling for Tanya—and that new element was keen curiosity, keen and cold as a steel knife.

"Mates! To-day the time's up!" our baker said to us one morning, as he set to work.

We were well aware of it without his reminder; but still we were thrilled.

"Look at her. She'll be here directly," suggested the baker.

One of us cried out in a troubled voice, "Why! as though one could notice anything!"

And again an eager, noisy discussion sprang up among us. To-day we were about to prove how pure and spotless was the vessel into which we had poured all that was best in us. This morning, for the first time, it became clear to us, that we really were playing a great game; that we might, indeed, through the exaction of this proof of purity, lose our divinity altogether.

During the whole of the intervening fortnight we had heard that Tanya was persistently followed by the soldier, but not one of us had thought of asking her how she had behaved towards him. And she came every morning to fetch her kringels, and was the same towards us as ever.

This morning, too, we heard her voice outside: "You poor prisoners! Here I am!"

We opened the door, and when she came in we all remained, contrary to our usual custom, silent. Our eyes fixed on her, we did not know how to speak to her, what to ask her. And there we stood in front of her, a gloomy, silent crowd. She seemed to be surprised at this unusual reception; suddenly we saw her turn white, and become uneasy, then she asked, in a choking voice: "Why are you—like this?"

"And you?" the baker flung at her, grimly, never taking his eyes off her.

"What am I?"

"N—nothing."

"Well, then, give me quickly the little kringels."

Never before had she bidden us hurry.

"There's plenty of time," said the baker, not stirring, and not removing his eyes from her face.

Then, suddenly, she turned round and disappeared through the door.

The baker took his shovel and said, calmly turning away towards the oven:

"Well, that settles it! But a soldier! a common beast like that—a low cur!"

Like a flock of sheep we all pressed round the table, sat down silently, and began listlessly to work. Soon, however, one of us remarked:

"Perhaps, after all—"

"Shut up!" shouted the baker.

We were all convinced that he was a man of judgment, a man who knew more than we did about things. And at the sound of his voice we were convinced of the soldier's victory, and our spirits became sad and downcast.

At twelve o'clock—whilst we were eating our dinners—the soldier came in. He was as clean and as smart as ever, and looked at us—as usual—straight in the eyes. But we were all awkward in looking at him.

"Now then, honoured sirs, would you like me to show you a soldier's quality?" He said, chuckling proudly.

"Go out into the passage, and look through the crack—do you understand?"

We went into the passage, and stood all pushing against one another, squeezed up to the cracks of the wooden partition of the passage that looked into the yard. We had not to wait long. Very soon Tanya, with hurried footsteps and a careworn face, walked across the yard, jumping over the puddles of melting snow and mud: she disappeared into the store cellar. Then whistling, and not hurrying himself, the soldier followed in the same direction. His hands were thrust in his pockets; his moustaches were quivering.

Rain was falling, and we saw how its drops fell into the puddles, and the puddles were wrinkled by them. The day was damp and grey—a very dreary day. Snow still lay on the roofs, but on the ground dark patches of mud had begun to appear. And the snow on the roofs too was covered by a layer of brownish dirt. The rain fell slowly with a depressing sound. It was cold and disagreeable for us waiting.

The first to come out of the store cellar was the soldier; he walked slowly across the yard, his moustaches twitching, his hands in his pockets—the same as always.

Then—Tanya, too, came out. Her eyes—her

eyes were radiant with joy and happiness, and her lips—were smiling. And she walked as though in a dream, staggering, with unsteady steps.

We could not bear this quietly. All of us at once rushed to the door, dashed out into the yard and—hissed at her, reviled her viciously, loudly, wildly.

She started at seeing us, and stood as though rooted in the mud under her feet. We formed a ring round her; and malignantly, without restraint, abused her with vile words, said shameful things to her.

We did this not loudly, not hurriedly, seeing that she could not get away, that she was hemmed in by us, and we could deride her to our hearts' content. I don't know why, but we did not beat her. She stood in the midst of us, and turned her head this way and that, as she heard our insults. And we—more and more violently flung at her the filth and venom of our words.

The colour had left her face. Her blue eyes, so happy a moment before, opened wide, her bosom heaved, and her lips quivered.

We in a ring round her avenged ourselves on

her as though she had robbed us. She belonged to us, we had lavished on her our best, and though that best was a beggar's crumb, still we were twenty-six, she was one, and so there was no pain we could give her equal to her guilt! How we insulted her! She was still mute, still gazed at us with wild eyes, and a shiver ran all over her.

We laughed, roared, yelled. Other people ran up from somewhere and joined us. One of us pulled Tanya by the sleeve of her blouse.

Suddenly her eyes flashed; deliberately she raised her hands to her head and straightening her hair she said loudly but calmly, straight in our faces:

"Ah, you miserable prisoners!"

And she walked straight at us, walked as directly as though we had not been before her, as though we were not blocking her way.

And hence it was that no one did actually prevent her passing.

Walking out of our ring, without turning round, she said loudly and with indescribable contempt:

"Ah you scum—brutes."

And—was gone.

We were left in the middle of the yard, in the rain, under the grey sky without the sun.

Then we went mutely away to our damp stone cellar. As before—the sun never peeped in at our windows, and Tanya came no more!

TCHELKASH.

AN EPISODE.

Darkened by the dust of the dock, the blue southern sky is murky; the burning sun looks duskily into the greenish sea, as though through a thin grey veil. It can find no reflection in the water, continually cut up by the strokes of oars, the screws of steamers, the deep sharp keels of Turkish feluccas and other sailing vessels, that pass in all directions, ploughing up the crowded harbour, where the free waves of the sea, pent up within granite walls, and crushed under the vast weights that glide over its crests, beat upon the sides of the ships and on the bank; beat and complain, churned up into foam and fouled with all sorts of refuse.

The jingle of the anchor chains, the rattle of the links of the trucks that bring down the cargoes, the metallic clank of sheets of iron falling on the stone pavement, the dull thud of wood, the creaking of the carts plying for hire, the whistles of the steamers, piercingly shrill and hoarsely roaring, the shouts of dock labourers, sailors, and customs officers,—all these sounds melt into the deafening symphony of the working day, that hovering uncertainly hangs over the harbour, as though afraid to float upwards and be lost. And fresh waves of sound continually rise up from the earth to join it; deep, grumbling, sullen reverberations setting all around quaking; shrill, menacing notes that pierce the ear and the dusty, sultry air.

The granite, the iron, the wood, the harbour pavement, the ships and the men—all swelled the mighty strains of this frenzied, impassioned hymn to Mercury. But the voices of men, scarcely audible in it, were weak and ludicrous. And the men, too, themselves, the first source of all that uproar, were ludicrous and pitiable: their little figures, dusty, tattered, nimble, bent under the weight of goods that lay on their backs, under the weight of cares that drove them hither and thither, in the clouds of dust, in the sea of sweltering heat and din, were so trivial and small in comparison with the colossal iron monsters, the mountains of bales, the thundering railway trucks and all that they had created. Their own creation had enslaved them, and stolen away their individual life.

As they lay letting off steam, the heavy giant steamers whistled or hissed, or seemed to heave deep sighs, and in every sound that came from them could be heard the mocking note of ironical contempt for the grey, dusty shapes of men, crawling about their decks and filling their deep holds with the fruits of their slavish toil. Ludicrous and pitiable were the long strings of dock labourers bearing on their backs thousands of tons of bread, and casting it into the iron bellies of the ships to gain a few pounds of that same bread to fill their own bellies—for their worse luck not made of iron, but alive to the pangs of hunger. The men, tattered, drenched with sweat, made dull by weariness, and din and heat; and the mighty machines, created by those men, shining, well-fed, serene, in the sunshine; machines which in the last resort are, after all, not set in motion by steam, but by the muscles and blood of their creators—in this contrast was a whole poem of cruel and frigid irony.

The clamour oppressed the spirit, the dust

fretted the nostrils and blinded the eyes, the sweltering heat baked and exhausted the body, and everything—buildings, men, pavement—seemed strained, breaking, ready to burst, losing patience, on the verge of exploding into some immense catastrophe, some outbreak, after which one would be able to breathe freely and easily in the air refreshed by it. On the earth there would be quietness; and that dusty uproar, deafening, fretting the nerves, driving one to melancholy frenzy, would vanish; and in town, and sea and sky, it would be still and clear and pleasant. But that was only seeming. It seemed so because man has not yet grown weary of hoping for better things, and the longing to feel free is not dead in him.

Twelve times there rang out the regular musical peal of the bell. When the last brazen clang had died away, the savage orchestra of toil had already lost half its volume. A minute later it had passed into a dull repining grumble. Now the voices of men and the splash of the sea could be heard more clearly. The dinner-hour had come.

I.

When the dock labourers, knocking off work, had scattered about the dock in noisy groups, buying various edibles from the women hawking food, and were settling themselves to dinner in shady corners on the pavement, there walked into their midst Grishka Tchelkash, an old hunted wolf, well known to all the dock population as a hardened drunkard and a bold and dexterous thief. He was barefoot and bareheaded, clad in old, threadbare, shoddy breeches, in a dirty print shirt, with a torn collar that displayed his mobile, dry, angular bones tightly covered with brown skin. From the ruffled state of his black, slightly grizzled hair and the dazed look on his keen, predatory face, it was evident that he had only just waked up. There was a straw sticking in one brown moustache, another straw clung to the scrubby bristles of his shaved left cheek, and behind his ear he had stuck a little, freshly-picked twig of lime. Long, bony, rather stooping, he paced slowly over the flags, and turning his hooked, rapacious-looking nose from side to side, he cast sharp glances about him, his cold grey eyes shining, as he scanned one after another among the dock labourers. His thick and long brown moustaches were continually twitching like a cat's whiskers, while he rubbed his hands behind his back, nervously clenching the long, crooked, clutching fingers. Even here, among hundreds of striking-looking, tattered vagabonds like himself, he attracted attention at once from his resemblance to a vulture of the steppes, from his hungry-looking thinness, and from that peculiar gait of his, as though pouncing down on his prey, so smooth and easy in appearance, but inwardly intent and alert, like the flight of the keen, nervous bird he resembled.

As he reached one of the groups of ragged dockers, reclining in the shade of a stack of coal baskets, there rose to meet him a thick-set young man, with purple blotches on his dull face and scratches on his neck, unmistakeable traces of a recent thrashing. He got up and walked beside Tchelkash, saying, in an undertone:

"The dock officers have got wind of the two cases of goods. They're on the look-out. D'ye hear, Grishka?"

"What then?" queried Tchelkash, coolly measuring him with his eyes.

"How 'what then?' They're on the look-out, I say. That's all."

"Did they ask for me to help them look?"

And with an acrid smile Tchelkash looked towards the storehouse of the Volunteer Fleet.

"You go to the devil!"

His companion turned away.

"Ha, wait a bit! Who's been decorating you like that? Why, what a sight they have made of your signboard! Have you seen Mishka here?"

"I've not seen him this long while!" the other shouted, and hastily went back to his companions.

Tchelkash went on further, greeted by everyone as a familiar figure. But he, usually so lively and sarcastic, was unmistakeably out of humour to-day, and made short and abrupt replies to all enquiries.

From behind a pile of goods emerged a customs-house officer, a dark green, dusty figure, of military erectness. He barred the way for Tchelkash, standing before him in a challenging attitude, his left hand clutching the hilt of his dirk, while with his right he tried to seize Tchelkash by the collar.

"Stop! Where are you going?"

Tchelkash drew back a step, raised his eyes, looked at the official, and smiled drily.

The red, good-humouredly crafty face of the official, in its attempt to assume a menacing air, puffed and grew round and purple, while the brows scowled, the eyes rolled, and the effect was very comic.

"You've been told—don't you dare come into the dock, or I'll break your ribs! And you're here again!" the man roared, threateningly.

"How d'ye do, Semyonitch! it's a long while since we've seen each other," Tchelkash greeted him calmly, holding out his hand.

"Thankful never to see you again! Get along, get along!"

But yet Semyonitch took the outstretched hand.

"You tell me this," Tchelkash went on, his gripping fingers still keeping their hold of Semyonitch's hand, and shaking it with friendly familiarity, "haven't you seen Mishka?"

"Mishka, indeed, who's Mishka? I don't know any Mishka. Get along, mate! or the inspector'll see you, he'll——"

"The red-haired fellow that I worked with

last time on the 'Kostroma'?" Tchelkash persisted.

"That you steal with, you'd better say. He's been taken to the hospital, your Mishka; his foot was crushed by an iron bar. Go away, mate, while you're asked to civilly, go away, or I'll chuck you out by the scruff of your neck."

"A-ha, that's like you! And you say—you don't know Mishka! But I say, why are you so cross, Semyonitch?"

"I tell you, Grishka, don't give me any of your jaw. Go—o!"

The official began to get angry and, looking from side to side, tried to pull his hand away from Tchelkash's firm grip. Tchelkash looked calmly at him from under his thick eyebrows, smiled behind his moustache, and not letting go of his hand, went on talking.

"Don't hurry me. I'll just have my chat out with you, and then I'll go. Come, tell us how you're getting on; wife and children quite well?" And with a spiteful gleam in his eyes, he added, showing his teeth in a mocking grin: "I've been meaning to pay you a call for ever so long, but I've not had the time, I'm always drinking, you see."

"Now—now then—you drop that! You—none of your jokes, you bony devil. I'm in earnest, my man. So you mean you're coming stealing in the houses and the streets?"

"What for? Why, there's goods enough here to last our time—for you and me. By God, there's enough, Semyonitch! So you've been filching two cases of goods, eh? Mind, Semyonitch, you'd better look out! You'll get caught one day!"

Enraged by Tchelkash's insolence, Semyonitch turned blue, and struggled, spluttering and trying to say something. Tchelkash let go of his hand, and with complete composure strode back to the dock gates. The customs-house officer followed him, swearing furiously. Tchelkash grew more cheerful; he whistled shrilly through his teeth, and thrusting his hands in his breeches pockets, walked with the deliberate gait of a man of leisure, firing off to right and to left biting jeers and jests. He was followed by retorts in the same vein.

"I say, Grishka, what good care they do take of you! Made your inspection, eh?" shouted one out of a group of dockers, who had finished dinner and were lying on the ground, resting.

"I'm barefoot, so here's Semyonitch watching that I shouldn't graze my foot on anything," answered Tchelkash.

They reached the gates. Two soldiers felt Tchelkash all over, and gave him a slight shove into the street.

"Don't let him go!" wailed Semyonitch, who had stayed behind in the dockyard.

Tchelkash crossed the road and sat down on a stone post opposite the door of the inn. From the dock gates rolled rumbling an endless string of laden carts. To meet them, rattled empty carts, with their drivers jolting up and down in them. The dock vomited howling din and biting dust, and set the earth quaking.

Tchelkash, accustomed to this frenzied uproar, and roused by his scene with Semyonitch, felt in excellent spirits. Before him lay the attractive prospect of a substantial haul, which would call for some little exertion and a great deal of dexterity; Tchelkash was confident that he had plenty of the latter, and, half-closing his eyes, dreamed of how he would indulge to-morrow morning when the business would be over and the notes would be rustling in his pocket. Then he thought of his comrade, Mishka, who would have been very useful that night, if he had not hurt his foot; Tchelkash swore to himself, thinking that, all alone, without Mishka, maybe he'd hardly manage it all. What sort of night would it be? Tchelkash looked at the sky, and along the street.

Half-a-dozen paces from him, on the flagged pavement, there sat, leaning against a stone post, a young fellow in a coarse blue linen shirt, and breeches of the same, in plaited bark shoes, and a torn, reddish cap. Near him lay a little bag, and a scythe without a handle, with a wisp of hay twisted round it and carefully tied with string. The youth was broad-shouldered, squarely-built, flaxen-headed, with a sunburnt and weather-beaten face, and big blue eyes that stared with confident simplicity at Tchelkash.

Tchelkash grinned at him, put out his tongue, and making a fearful face, stared persistently at him with wide-open eyes.

The young fellow at first blinked in bewilderment, but then, suddenly bursting into a guffaw, shouted through his laughter: "Oh! you funny chap!" and half getting up from the ground, rolled clumsily from his post to Tchelkash's, upsetting his bag into the dust, and knocking the heel of his scythe on the stone

"Eh, mate, you've been on the spree, one can see!" he said to Tchelkash, pulling at his trousers.

"That's so, suckling, that's so indeed!" Tchelkash admitted frankly; he took at once to this healthy, simple-hearted youth, with his childish clear eyes. "Been off mowing, eh?"

"To be sure! You've to mow a verst to earn ten copecks! It's a poor business! Folks—in masses! Men had come tramping from the famine parts. They've knocked down the prices, go where you will. Sixty copecks they paid in Kuban. And in years gone by, they do say, it was three, and four, and five roubles."

"In years gone by! Why, in years gone by, for the mere sight of a Russian they paid three roubles out that way. Ten years ago I used to make a regular trade of it. One would go to a settlement,—"I'm a Russian," one said—and they'd come and gaze at you at once, touch you, wonder at you and—you'd get three roubles. And they'd give you food and drink—stay as long as you like!"

As the youth listened to Tchelkash, at first his

mouth dropped open, his round face expressing bewildered rapture; then, grasping the fact that this tattered fellow was romancing, he closed his lips with a smack and guffawed. Tchelkash kept a serious face, hiding a smile in his moustache.

"You funny chap, you chaff away as though it were the truth, and I listen as if it were a bit of news! No, upon my soul, in years gone by—"

"Why, and didn't I say so? To be sure, I'm telling you how in years gone by—"

"Go on!" the lad waved his hand. "A cobbler, eh? or a tailor? or what are you?"

"I?" Tchelkash queried, and after a moment's thought, he said: "I'm a fisherman."

"A fi-isherman! Really? You catch fish?"

"Why fish? Fishermen about here don't catch fish only. They fish more for drowned men, old anchors, sunk ships,—everything! There are hooks on purpose for all that."

"Go on! That sort of fishermen, maybe, that sing of themselves:

We cast our nets
Over banks that are dry
Over storerooms and pantries!"

"Why, have you seen any of that sort?" enquired Tchelkash, looking scoffingly at him and thinking that this nice youth was very stupid.

"No, seen them I haven't! I've heard tell."

"Do you like them?"

"Like them? May be. They're all right, fine bold chaps—free."

"And what's—freedom to you? Do you care for freedom?

"Well, I should think so! Be your own master, go where you please, do as you like. To be sure! If you know how to behave yourself, and you've nothing weighing upon you,—it's first rate. Enjoy yourself all you can, only be mindful of God."

Tchelkash spat contemptuously, and turning away from the youth, dropped the conversation.

"Here's my case now," the latter began with sudden animation. "As my father's dead, my bit of land's small, my mother's old, all the land's sucked dry, what am I to do? I must live. And how? There's no telling.

"Am I to marry into some well-to-do house? I'd be glad to, if only they'd let their daughter have her share apart.

"Not a bit of it, the devil of a father-in-law won't consent to that. And so I shall have to slave for him—for ever so long—for years. A nice state of things, you know!

"But if I could earn a hundred or a hundred-and-fifty roubles, I could stand on my own feet, and look askance at old Antip, and tell him straight out! Will you give Marfa her share apart? No? all right then! Thank God she's not the only girl in the village. And I should be, I mean, quite free and independent.

"Ah, yes!" the young man sighed. "But as 'tis, there's nothing for it, but to marry and live at my father-in-law's. I was thinking I'd go, d'ye see, to Kuban, and make some two hundred roubles—straight off! Be a gentleman! But there, it was no go! It didn't come off. Well, I suppose I'll have to work for my father-in-law! Be a day-labourer. For I'll never manage on my own bit—not anyhow. Heigh-ho!"

The lad extremely disliked the idea of bondage to his future father-in-law. His face positively darkened and looked gloomy. He shifted clumsily on the ground and drew Tchelkash out of the reverie into which he had sunk during his speech.

Tchelkash felt that he had no inclination now to talk to him, yet he asked him another question: "Where are you going now?"

"Why, where should I go? Home, to be sure."

"Well, mate, I couldn't be sure of that, you might be on your way to Turkey."

"To Tu-urkey!" drawled the youth. "Why, what good Christian ever goes there! Well I never!"

"Oh, you fool!" sighed Tchelkash, and again he turned away from his companion, conscious this time of a positive disinclination to waste another word on him. This stalwart village lad roused some feeling in him. It was a vague feeling of annoyance, that grew instinctively, stirred deep down in his heart, and hindered him from concentrating himself on the consideration of all that he had to do that night.

The lad he had thus reviled muttered something, casting occasionally a dubious glance at Tchelkash. His cheeks were comically puffed out, his lips parted, and his eyes were screwed up and blinking with extreme rapidity. He had obviously not expected so rapid and insulting a termination to his conversation with this long-whiskered ragamuffin. The ragamuffin took no further notice of him. He whistled dreamily, sitting on the stone post, and beating time on it with his bare, dirty heel.

The young peasant wanted to be quits with him.

"Hi, you there, fisherman! Do you often get tipsy like this?" he was beginning, but at the same instant the fisherman turned quickly towards him, and asked:

"I say, suckling! Would you like a job to-night with me? Eh? Tell me quickly!"

"What sort of a job?" the lad asked, distrustfully.

"What! What I set you. We're going fishing. You'll row the boat."

"Well. Yes. All right. I don't mind a job. Only there's this. I don't want to get into a mess with you. You're so awfully deep. You're rather shady."

Tchelkash felt a scalding sensation in his breast, and with cold anger he said in a low voice:

"And you'd better hold your tongue, whatever you think, or I'll give you a tap on your nut that will make things light enough."

He jumped up from his post, tugged at his moustache with his left hand, while his sinewy right hand was clenched into a fist, hard as iron, and his eyes gleamed.

The youth was frightened. He looked quickly round him, and blinking uneasily, he, too, jumped up from the ground. Measuring one another with their eyes, they paused.

"Well?" Tchelkash queried, sullenly. He was boiling inwardly, and trembling at the affront dealt him by this young calf, whom he had despised while he talked to him, but now hated all at once because he had such clear blue eyes, such health, a sunburnt face, and broad, strong hands; because he had somewhere a village, a home in it, because a well-to-do peasant wanted him for a son-in-law, because of all his life, past and future, and most of all, because he—this babe compared with Tchelkash—dared to love freedom, which he could not appreciate, nor need. It is always unpleasant to see that a man one regards as baser or lower than oneself likes or hates the same things, and so puts himself on a level with oneself.

The young peasant looked at Tchelkash and saw in him an employer.

"Well," he began, "I don't mind. I'm glad of it. Why, it's work I'm looking for. I don't care whom I work for, you or any other man. I only meant that you don't look like a working man—a bit too—ragged. Oh, I know that may happen to anyone. Good Lord, as though I've never seen drunkards! Lots of them! and worse than you, too."

"All right, all right! Then you agree?" Tchelkash said more amicably.

"I? Ye-es! With pleasure! Name your terms."

"That's according to the job. As the job turns out. According to our catch, that's to say. Five roubles you may get. Do you see?

But now it was a question of money, and in that the peasant wished to be precise, and demanded the same exactness from his employer. His distrust and suspicion revived.

"That's not my way of doing business, mate! A bird in the hand for me."

Tchelkash threw himself into his part.

"Don't argue, wait a bit! Come into the restaurant."

And they went down the street side by side, Tchelkash with the dignified air of an employer, twisting his moustaches, the youth with an expression of absolute readiness to give way to him, but yet full of distrust and uneasiness.

"And what's your name?" asked Tchelkash.

"Gavrilo!" answered the youth.

When they had come into the dirty and smoky eating-house, and Tchelkash going up to the counter, in the familiar tone of an habitual customer, ordered a bottle of vodka, cabbage soup, a cut from the joint, and tea, and reckoning up his order, flung the waiter a brief "put it all down!" to which the waiter nodded in silence,—Gavrilo was at once filled with respect for this ragamuffin, his employer, who enjoyed here such an established and confident position.

"Well, now we'll have a bit of lunch and talk things over. You sit still, I'll be back in a minute."

He went out. Gavrilo looked round. The restaurant was in an underground basement; it was damp and dark, and reeked with the stifling fumes of vodka, tobacco-smoke, tar, and some acrid odour. Facing Gavrilo at another table sat a drunken man in the dress of a sailor, with a red beard, all over coal-dust and tar. Hiccupping every minute, he was droning a song all made up of broken and incoherent words, strangely sibilant and guttural sounds. He was unmistakeably not a Russian.

Behind him sat two Moldavian women, tattered, black-haired sunburnt creatures, who were chanting some sort of song, too, with drunken voices.

And from the darkness beyond emerged other figures, all strangely dishevelled, all half-drunk, noisy and restless.

Gavrilo felt miserable here alone. He longed for his employer to come back quickly. And the din in the eating-house got louder and louder. Growing shriller every second, it all melted into one note, and it seemed like the roaring of some monstrous beast, with hundreds of different throats, vaguely enraged, trying to struggle out of this damp hole and unable to find a way out to freedom. Gavrilo felt something intoxicating and oppressive creeping over him, over all his limbs, making his head reel, and his eyes grow dim, as they moved inquisitively about the eating-house.

Tchelkash came in, and they began eating and drinking and talking. At the third glass Gavrilo was drunk. He became lively and wanted to say something pleasant to his employer, who—the good fellow!—though he had done nothing for him yet, was entertaining him so agreeably. But the words which flowed in perfect waves to his throat, for some reason would not come from his tongue.

Tchelkash looked at him and smiled sarcastically, saying:

"You're screwed! Ugh—milksop!—with five glasses! how will you work?"

"Dear fellow!" Gavrilo melted into a drunken good-natured smile. "Never fear! I respect you! That is, look here! Let me kiss you! eh?"

"Come, come! A drop more!"

Gavrilo drank, and at last reached a condition when everything seemed waving up and down in regular undulations before his eyes. It was unpleasant and made him feel sick. His face wore an expression of childish bewilderment and foolish enthusiasm. Trying to say something, he smacked his lips absurdly and bellowed. Tchelkash, watching him intently, twisted his moustaches, and as though recollecting something, still smiled to himself, but morosely now and maliciously.

The eating-house roared with drunken clamour. The red-headed sailor was asleep, with his elbows on the table.

"Come, let's go then!" said Tchelkash, getting up. Gavrilo tried to get up, but could not, and with a vigorous oath, laughed a meaningless drunken laugh.

"Quite screwed!" said Tchelkash, sitting down again opposite him.

Gavrilo still guffawed, staring with dull eyes at his new employer. And the latter gazed at him intently, vigilantly and thoughtfully. He saw before him a man whose life had fallen into his wolfish clutches. He, Tchelkash, felt that he had the power to do with it as he pleased. He could rend it like a card, and he could help to set it on a firm footing in its peasant framework. He revelled in feeling himself master of another man, and thought that never would this peasant-lad drink of such a cup as destiny had given him, Tchelkash, to drink. And he envied this young life and pitied it, sneered at it, and was even troubled over it, picturing to himself how it might again fall into such hands as his.

And all these feelings in the end melted in Tchelkash into one—a fatherly sense of proprietorship in him. He felt sorry for the boy, and the boy was necessary to him. Then Tchelkash took Gavrilo under the arms, and giving him a slight shove behind with his knee, got him out into the yard of the eating-house, where he put him on the ground in the shade of a stack of wood, then he sat down beside him and lighted his pipe. Gavrilo shifted about a little, muttered, and dropped asleep.

II.

"Come, ready?" Tchelkash asked in a low voice of Gavrilo, who was busy doing something to the oars.

"In a minute! The rowlock here's unsteady, can I just knock it in with the oar?"

"No—no! Not a sound! Push it down harder with your hand, it'll go in of itself."

They were both quietly getting out a boat, which was tied to the stern of one of a whole flotilla of oak-laden barges, and big Turkish feluccas, half unloaded, half still full of palm-oil, sandal wood, and thick trunks of cypress.

The night was dark, thick strata of ragged clouds were moving across the sky, and the sea was quiet, black, and thick as oil. It wafted a damp and salt aroma, and splashed caressingly on the sides of the vessels and the banks, setting Tchelkash's boat lightly rocking. There were boats all round them. At a long distance from the shore rose from the sea the dark outlines of vessels, thrusting up into the dark sky their pointed masts with various coloured lights at their tops. The sea reflected the lights, and was spotted with masses of yellow, quivering patches. This was very beautiful on the velvety bosom of the soft, dull black water, so rhythmically, mightily breathing. The sea slept the sound, healthy sleep of a workman, wearied out by his day's toil.

"We're off!" said Gavrilo, dropping the oars into the water.

"Yes!" With a vigorous turn of the rudder Tchelkash drove the boat into a strip of water between two barques, and they darted rapidly over the smooth surface, that kindled into bluish phosphorescent light under the strokes of the oars. Behind the boat's stern lay a winding ribbon of this phosphorescence, broad and quivering.

"Well, how's your head, aching?" asked Tchelkash, smiling.

"Awfully! Like iron ringing. I'll wet it with some water in a minute."

"Why? You'd better wet your inside, that may get rid of it. You can do that at once." He held out a bottle to Gavrilo.

"Eh? Lord bless you!

There was a faint sound of swallowing.

"Aye! aye! like it? Enough!" Tchelkash stopped him.

The boat darted on again, noiselessly and lightly threading its way among the vessels. All at once, they emerged from the labyrinth of ships, and the sea, boundless, mute, shining and rhythmically breathing, lay open before them, stretching far into the distance, where there rose out of its waters masses of storm clouds, some lilac-blue with fluffy yellow edges, and some greenish like the colour of the seawater, or those dismal, leaden-coloured clouds that cast such heavy, dreary shadows, oppressing mind and soul. They crawled slowly after one another, one melting into another, one overtaking another, and there was something weird in this slow procession of soulless masses. It seemed as though there, at the sea's rim, they were a countless multitude, that they would for ever crawl thus sluggishly over the sky, striving with dull malignance to hinder it from peeping at the sleeping sea with its millions of golden eyes, the various coloured, vivid stars, that shine so dreamily and stir high hopes in all who love their pure, holy light. Over the sea hovered the vague, soft sound of its drowsy breathing.

"The sea's fine, eh?" asked Tchelkash.

"It's all right! Only I feel scared on it," answered Gavrilo, pressing the oars vigorously and evenly through the water. The water faintly gurgled and splashed under the strokes of his long oars, splashed glittering with the warm, bluish, phosphorescent light.

"Scared! What a fool!" Tchelkash muttered, discontentedly.

He, the thief and cynic, loved the sea. His effervescent, nervous nature, greedy after impressions, was never weary of gazing at that dark expanse, boundless, free, and mighty. And it hurt him to hear such an answer to his question about the beauty of what he loved. Sitting in the stern, he cleft the water with his oar, and looked on ahead quietly, filled with desire to glide far on this velvety surface, not soon to quit it.

On the sea there always rose up in him a

broad, warm feeling, that took possession of his whole soul, and somewhat purified it from the sordidness of daily life. He valued this, and loved to feel himself better out here in the midst of the water and the air, where the cares of life, and life itself, always lose, the former their keenness, the latter its value.

"But where's the tackle? Eh?" Gavrilo asked suspiciously all at once, peering into the boat.

Tchelkash started.

"Tackle? I've got it in the stern."

"Why, what sort of tackle is it?" Gavrilo enquired again with surprised suspicion in his tone.

"What sort? lines and—" But Tchelkash felt ashamed to lie to this boy, to conceal his real plans, and he was sorry to lose what this peasant-lad had destroyed in his heart by this question. He flew into a rage. That scalding bitterness he knew so well rose in his breast and his throat, and impressively, cruelly, and malignantly he said to Gavrilo:

"You're sitting here—and I tell you, you'd better sit quiet. And not poke your nose into what's not your business. You've been hired to row, and you'd better row. But if you can't keep your tongue from wagging, it will be a bad look-out for you. Dy'e see?"

For a minute the boat quivered and stopped. The oars rested in the water, setting it foaming, and Gavrilo moved uneasily on his seat.

"Row!"

A sharp oath rang out in the air. Gavrilo swung the oars. The boat moved with rapid, irregular jerks, noisily cutting the water.

"Steady!"

Tchelkash got up from the stern, still holding the oars in his hands, and peering with his cold eyes into the pale and twitching face of Gavrilo. Crouching forward Tchelkash was like a cat on the point of springing. There was the sound of angry gnashing of teeth.

"Who's calling?" rang out a surly shout from the sea.

"Now, you devil, row! quietly with the oars! I'll kill you, you cur. Come, row! One, two! There! you only make a sound! I'll cut your throat!" hissed Tchelkash.

"Mother of God—Holy Virgin—" muttered Gavrilo, shaking and numb with terror and exertion.

The boat turned smoothly and went back

towards the harbour, where the lights gathered more closely into a group of many colours and the straight stems of masts could be seen.

"Hi! Who's shouting?" floated across again. The voice was further off this time. Tchelkash grew calm again.

"It's yourself, friend, that's shouting!" he said in the direction of the shouts, and then he turned to Gavrilo, who was still muttering a prayer.

"Well, mate, you're in luck! If those devils had overtaken us, it would have been all over with you. D'you see? I'd have had you over in a trice—to the fishes!

Now, when Tchelkash was speaking quietly and even good-humouredly, Gavrilo, still shaking with terror, besought him:

"Listen, forgive me! For Christ's sake, I beg you, let me go! Put me on shore somewhere! Aïe-aïe-aïe! I'm done for entirely! Come, think of God, let me go! What am I to you? I can't do it! I've never been used to such things. It's the first time. Lord! Why, I shall be lost! How did you get round me, mate? eh? It's a shame of you! Why, you're ruining a man's life! Such doings."

"What doings?" Tchelkash asked grimly. "Eh? Well, what doings?"

He was amused by the youth's terror, and he enjoyed it and the sense that he, Tchelkash, was a terrible person.

"Shady doings, mate. Let me go, for God's sake! What am I to you? eh? Good—dear—!"

"Hold your tongue, do! If you weren't wanted, I shouldn't have taken you. Do you understand? So, shut up!"

"Lord!" Gavrilo sighed sobbing.

"Come, come! you'd better mind!" Tchelkash cut him short.

But Gavrilo by now could not restrain himself, and quietly sobbing, he wept, sniffed, and writhed in his seat, yet rowed vigorously, desperately. The boat shot on like an arrow. Again dark hulks of ships rose up on their way and the boat was again lost among them, winding like a wolf in the narrow lanes of water between them.

"Here, you, listen! If anyone asks you anything,—hold your tongue, if you want to get off alive! Do you see?

"Oh—oh!" Gavrilo sighed hopelessly in answer to the grim advice, and bitterly he added: "I'm a lost man!"

"Don't howl!" Tchelkash whispered impressively.

This whisper deprived Gavrilo of all power of grasping anything and transformed him into a senseless automaton, wholly absorbed in a chill presentiment of calamity. Mechanically he lowered the oars into the water, threw himself back, drew them out and dropped them in again, all the while staring blankly at his plaited shoes. The waves splashed against the vessels with a sort of menace, a sort of warning in their drowsy sound that terrified him. The dock was reached. From its granite wall came the sound of men's voices, the splash of water, singing, and shrill whistles.

"Stop!" whispered Tchelkash. "Give over rowing! Push along with your hands on the wall! Quietly, you devil!"

Gavrilo, clutching at the slippery stone, pushed the boat alongside the wall. The boat moved without a sound, sliding alongside the green, shiny stone.

"Stop! Give me the oars! Give them here. Where's your passport? In the bag? Give me the bag! Come, give it here quickly! That, my dear fellow, is so you shouldn't run off. You won't run away now. Without oars you might have got off somehow, but without a passport you'll be afraid to. Wait here! But mind—if you squeak—to the bottom of the sea you go!

And, all at once, clinging on to something with his hands, Tchelkash rose in the air and vanished on to the wall.

Gavrilo shuddered. It had all happened so quickly. He felt as though the cursed weight and horror that had crushed him in the presence of this thin thief with his moustaches was loosened and rolling off him. Now to run! And breathing freely, he looked round him. On his left rose a black hulk, without masts, a sort of huge coffin, mute, untenanted, and desolate. Every splash of the water on its sides awakened a hollow, resonant echo within it, like a heavy sigh.

On the right the damp stone wall of the quay trailed its length, winding like a heavy, chill serpent. Behind him, too, could be seen black blurs of some sort, while in front, in the opening between the wall and the side of that coffin, he could see the sea, a silent waste, with the storm-clouds crawling above it. Everything was cold, black, malignant. Gavrilo felt panic-stricken. This terror was worse than the terror inspired in him by Tchelkash ; it penetrated into Gavrilo's bosom with icy keenness, huddled him into a cowering mass, and kept him nailed to his seat in the boat.

All around was silent. Not a sound but the sighs of the sea, and it seemed as though this silence would instantly be rent by something fearful, furiously loud, something that would shake the sea to its depths, tear apart these heavy flocks of clouds on the sky, and scatter all these black ships. The clouds were crawling over the sky as dismally as before; more of them still rose up out of the sea, and, gazing at the sky, one might believe that it, too, was a sea, but a sea in agitation, and grown petrified in its agitation, laid over that other sea beneath, that was so drowsy, serene, and smooth. The clouds were like waves, flinging themselves with curly grey crests down upon the earth and into the abysses of space, from which they were torn again by the wind, and tossed back upon the rising billows of cloud, that were not yet hidden under the greenish foam of their furious agitation.

Gavrilo felt crushed by this gloomy stillness and beauty, and felt that he longed to see his master come back quickly. And how was it that he lingered there so long? The time passed slowly, more slowly than those clouds crawled over the sky. And the stillness grew more malignant as time went on. From the wall of the quay came the sound of splashing, rustling, and something like whispering. It seemed to Gavrilo that he would die that moment.

"Hi! Asleep? Hold it! Carefully!" sounded the hollow voice of Tchelkash.

From the wall something cubical and heavy was let down. Gavrilo took it into the boat. Something else like it followed. Then across the wall stretched Tchelkash's long figure, the oars appeared from somewhere, Gavrilo's bag dropped at his feet, and Tchelkash, breathing heavily, settled himself in the stern.

Gavrilo gazed at him with a glad and timid smile.

"Tired?" he enquired.

"Bound to be that, calf! Come now, row your best! Put your back into it! You've earned good wages, mate. Half the job's done. Now we've only to slip under the devils' noses, and then you can take your money and go off to your Mashka. You've got a Mashka, I suppose, eh, kiddy?"

"N—no!" Gavrilo strained himself to the utmost, working his chest like a pair of bellows, and his arms like steel springs. The water gurgled under the boat, and the blue streak behind the stern was broader now. Gavrilo was soaked through with sweat at once, but he still rowed on with all his might. After living through such terror twice that night, he dreaded now having to go through it a third time, and longed for one thing only—to make an end quickly of this accursed task, to get on to land, and to run away from this man, before he really did kill him, or get him into prison. He resolved not to speak to him about anything, not to contradict him, to do all he told him, and, if he should succeed in getting successfully quit of him, to pay for a thanksgiving service to be said to-morrow to Nikolai the Wonder-worker. A passionate prayer was ready to burst out from his bosom. But he restained himself, puffed like a steamer, and was silent, glancing from under his brows at Tchelkash.

The latter, with his lean, long figure bent forward like a bird about to take flight, stared into the darkness ahead of the boat with his hawk eyes, and turning his rapacious, hooked nose from side to side, gripped with one hand the rudder handle, while with the other he twirled his moustache, that was continually quivering with smiles. Tchelkash was pleased with his success, with himself, and with this youth, who had been so frightened of him and had been turned into his slave. He had a vision of unstinted dissipation to-morrow, while now he enjoyed the sense of his strength, which had enslaved this young, fresh lad. He watched how he was toiling, and felt sorry for him, wanted to encourage him.

"Eh!" he said softly, with a grin. "Were you awfully scared? eh?"

"Oh, no!" sighed Gavrilo, and he cleared his throat.

"But now you needn't work so at the oars. Easy off! There's only one place now to pass. Rest a bit.

Gavrilo obediently paused, rubbed the sweat off his face with the sleeve of his shirt, and dropped the oars again into the water.

"Now, row more slowly, so that the water

shouldn't bubble. We've only the gates to pass. Softly, softly. For they're serious people here, mate. They might take a pop at one in a minute. They'd give you such a bump on your forehead, you wouldn't have time to call out."

The boat now crept along over the water almost without a sound. Only from the oars dripped blue drops of water, and when they trickled into the sea, a blue patch of light was kindled for a minute where they fell. The night had become still warmer and more silent. The sky was no longer like a sea in turmoil, the clouds were spread out and covered it with a smooth, heavy canopy that hung low over the water and did not stir. And the sea was still more calm and black, and stronger than ever was the warm salt smell from it.

"Ah, if only it would rain!" whispered Tchelkash. "We could get through then, behind a curtain as it were."

On the right and the left of the boat, like houses rising out of the black water, stood barges, black, motionless, and gloomy. On one of them moved a light; someone was walking up and down with a lantern. The sea stroked their sides with a hollow sound of supplication, and they responded with an echo, cold and resonant, as though unwilling to yield anything.

"The coastguards!" Tchelkash whispered hardly above a breath.

From the moment when he had bidden him row more slowly, Gavrilo had again been overcome by that intense agony of expectation. He craned forward into the darkness, and he felt as though he were growing bigger; his bones and sinews were strained with a dull ache, his head, filled with a single idea, ached, the skin on his back twitched, and his legs seemed pricked with sharp chill little pins and needles. His eyes ached from the strain of gazing into the darkness, whence he expected every instant something would spring up and shout to them: "Stop, thieves!"

Now when Tchelkash whispered: "the coastguards!" Gavrilo shuddered, and one intense, burning idea passed through him, and thrilled his overstrained nerves; he longed to cry out, to call men to his aid. He opened his mouth, and half rose from his seat, squared his chest, drew in a full draught of breath—and opened his mouth—but suddenly, struck down by a terror that smote him like a whip, he shut his eyes and rolled forward off his seat.

Far away on the horizon, ahead of the boat, there rose up out of the black water of the sea a huge fiery blue sword; it rose up, cleaving the darkness of night, its blade glided through the clouds in the sky, and lay, a broad blue streak on the bosom of the sea. It lay there, and in the streak of its light there sprang up out of the darkness ships unseen till then, black and mute, shrouded in the thick night mist. It seemed as though they had lain long at the bottom of the sea, dragged down by the mighty hands of the tempest; and now behold they had been drawn up by the power and at the will of this blue fiery sword, born of the sea—had been drawn up to gaze upon the sky and all that was above the water. Their rigging wrapped about the masts and looked like clinging seaweeds, that had risen from the depths with these black giants caught in their snares. And it rose upwards again from the sea, this strange blue sword,—rose, cleft the night again, and again fell down in another direction. And again, where it lay, there rose up out of the dark the outlines of vessels, unseen before.

Tchelkash's boat stopped and rocked on the

water, as though in uncertainty. Gavrilo lay at the bottom, his face hidden in his hands, until Tchelkash poked him with an oar and whispered furiously, but softly:

"Fool, it's the customs cruiser. That's the electric light! Get up, blockhead! Why, they'll turn the light on us in a minute! You'll be the ruin of yourself and me! Come!"

And at last, when a blow from the sharp end of the oar struck Gavrilo's head more violently, he jumped up, still afraid to open his eyes, sat down on the seat, and, fumbling for the oars, rowed the boat on.

"Quietly! I'll kill you! Didn't I tell you? There, quietly! Ah, you fool, damn you! What are you frightened of? Eh, pig face A lantern and a reflector, that's all it is. Softly with the oars! Mawkish devil! They turn the reflector this way and that way, and light up the sea, so as to see if there are folks like you and me afloat. To catch smugglers, they do it. They won't get us, they've sailed too far off. Don't be frightened, lad, they won't catch us. Now we——" Tchelkash looked triumphantly round. "It's over, we've rowed out of reach! Foo—o! Come, you're in luck."

Gavrilo sat mute; he rowed, and breathing hard, looked askance where that fiery sword still rose and sank. He was utterly unable to believe Tchelkash that it was only a lantern and a reflector. The cold blue brilliance, that cut through the darkness and made the sea gleam with silver light, had something about it inexplicable, portentous, and Gavrilo now sank into a sort of hypnotised, miserable terror. Some vague presentiment weighed aching on his breast. He rowed automatically, with pale face, huddled up as though expecting a blow from above, and there was no thought, no desire in him now, he was empty and soulless. The emotions of that night had swallowed up at last all that was human in him.

But Tchelkash was triumphant again; complete success! all anxiety at an end! His nerves, accustomed to strain, relaxed, returned to the normal. His moustaches twitched voluptuously, and there was an eager light in his eyes. He felt splendid, whistled through his teeth, drew in deep breaths of the damp sea air, looked about him in the darkness, and laughed good-naturedly when his eyes rested on Gavrilo.

The wind blew up and waked the sea into a sudden play of fine ripples. The clouds had become, as it were, finer and more transparent, but the sky was still covered with them. The wind, though still light, blew freely over the sea, yet the clouds were motionless and seemed plunged in some gray, dreary dream.

"Come, mate, pull yourself together! it's high time! Why, what a fellow you are; as though all the breath had been knocked out of your skin, and only a bag of bones was left! My dear fellow! It's all over now! Hey!"

It was pleasant to Gavrilo to hear a human voice, even though Tchelkash it was that spoke.

"I hear," he said, softly.

"Come, then, milksop. Come, you sit at the rudder and I'll take the oars, you must be tired!"

Mechanically Gavrilo changed places. When Tchelkash, as he changed places with him, glanced into his face, and noticed that he was staggering on his shaking legs, he felt still sorrier for the lad. He clapped him on the shoulder.

"Come, come, don't be scared! You've earned a good sum for it. I'll pay you richly, mate. Would you like twenty-five roubles, eh?"

"I—don't want anything. Only to be on shore."

Tchelkash waved his hand, spat, and fell to rowing, flinging the oars far back with his long arms.

The sea had waked up. It frolicked in little waves, bringing them forth, decking them with a fringe of foam, flinging them on one another, and breaking them up into tiny eddies. The foam, melting, hissed and sighed, and everything was filled with the musical plash and cadence. The darkness seemed more alive.

"Come, tell me," began Tchelkash, "you'll go home to the village, and you'll marry and begin digging the earth and sowing corn, your wife will bear you children, food won't be too plentiful, and so you'll grind away all your life. Well? Is there such sweetness in that?"

"Sweetness!" Gavrilo answered, timid and trembling, "what, indeed?"

The wind tore a rent in the clouds and through the gap peeped blue bits of sky, with one or two stars. Reflected in the frolicking sea, these stars danced on the waves, vanishing and shining out again.

"More to the right!" said Tchelkash. "Soon

we shall be there. Well, well! It's over. A haul that's worth it! See here. One night, and I've made five hundred roubles! Eh? What do you say to that?"

"Five hundred?" Gavrilo drawled, incredulously, but he was scared at once, and quickly asked, prodding the bundle in the boat with his foot. "Why, what sort of thing may this be?"

"That's silk. A costly thing. All that, if one sold it for its value, would fetch a thousand. But I sell cheap. Is that smart business?"

"I sa—ay?" Gavrilo drawled, dubiously. "If only I'd all that!" he sighed, recalling all at once the village, his poor little bit of land, his poverty, his mother, and all that was so far away and so near his heart; for the sake of which he had gone to seek work, for the sake of which he had suffered such agonies that night. A flood of memories came back to him of his village, running down the steep slope to the river and losing itself in a whole forest of birch trees, willows, and mountain-ashes. These memories breathed something warm into him and cheered him up. "Ah, it would be grand!" he sighed, mournfully.

"To be sure! I expect you'd bolt home by the railway! And wouldn't the girls make love to you at home, aye, aye! You could choose which you liked! You'd build yourself a house. No, the money, maybe, would hardly be enough for a house."

"That's true—it wouldn't do for a house. Wood's dear down our way."

"Well, never mind. You'd mend up the old one. How about a horse? Have you got one?'

"A horse? Yes, I have, but a wretched old thing it is."

"Well, then, you'd have a horse. A first-rate horse! A cow—sheep—fowls of all sorts. Eh?"

"Don't talk of it! If I only could! Oh, Lord! What a life I should have!"

"Aye, mate, your life would be first-rate. I know something about such things. I had a home of my own once. My father was one of the richest in the village."

Tchelkash rowed slowly. The boat danced on the waves that sportively splashed over its edge; it scarcely moved forward on the dark sea; which frolicked more and more gaily. The two men were dreaming, rocked on the water, and pensively looking around them. Tchelkash had turned Gavrilo's thoughts to his village with the aim of encouraging and reassuring him. At first he had talked grinning sceptically to himself under his moustaches, but afterwards, as he replied to his companion and reminded him of the joys of a peasant's life, which he had so long ago wearied of, had forgotten, and only now recalled, he was gradually carried away, and, instead of questioning the peasant youth about his village and its doings, unconsciously he dropped into describing it himself:

"The great thing in the peasant's life, mate, is its freedom! You're your own master. You've your own home—worth a farthing, maybe—but it's yours! You've your own land—only a handful the whole of it—but it's yours! Hens of your own, eggs, apples of your own! You're king on your own land! And then the regularity. You get up in the morning, you've work to do, in the spring one sort, in the summer another, in the autumn, in the winter—different again. Wherever you go, you've home to come back to! It's snug! There's peace! You're a king! Aren't you really?" Tchelkash concluded enthusiastically his long reckoning of the peasant's advantages and privileges, forgetting, somehow, his duties.

Gavrilo looked at him with curiosity, and he, too, warmed to the subject. During this conversation he had succeeded in forgetting with whom he had to deal, and he saw in his companion a peasant like himself—cemented to the soil for ever by the sweat of generations, and bound to it by the recollections of childhood—who had wilfully broken loose from it and from its cares, and was bearing the inevitable punishment for this abandonment.

"That's true, brother! Ah, how true it is! Look at you, now, what you've become away from the land! Aha! The land, brother, is like a mother, you can't forget it for long."

Tchelkash awaked from his reverie. He felt that scalding irritation in his chest, which always came as soon as his pride, the pride of the reckless vagrant, was touched by anyone, and especially by one who was of no value in his eyes.

"His tongue's set wagging! he said savagely, "you thought, maybe, I said all that in earnest. Never fear!"

"But, you strange fellow!"—Gavrilo began, overawed again—"Was I speaking of you?

Why, there's lots like you! Ah, what a lot of unlucky people in the people! Wanderers—"

"Take the oars, you sea-calf!" Tchelkash commanded briefly, for some reason holding back a whole torrent of furious abuse, which surged up into his throat.

They changed places again, and Tchelkash, as he crept across the boat to the stern, felt an intense desire to give Gavrilo a kick that would send him flying into the water, and at the same time could not pluck up courage to look him in the face.

The brief conversation dropped, but now Gavrilo's silence even was eloquent of the country to Tchelkash. He recalled the past, and forgot to steer the boat, which was turned by the current and floated away out to sea. The waves seemed to understand that this boat had missed its way, and played lightly with it, tossing it higher and higher, and kindling their gay blue light under its oars. While before Tchelkash's eyes floated pictures of the past, the far past, separated from the present by the whole barrier of eleven years of vagrant life. He saw himself a child, his village, his mother, a red-cheeked plump woman, with kindly grey eyes, his father, a red-bearded giant with a stern face. He saw himself betrothed, and saw his wife, black-eyed Anfisa, with her long hair, plump, mild, and good humoured; again himself a handsome soldier in the Guards; again his father, grey now and bent with toil, and his mother wrinkled and bowed to the ground; he saw, too, the picture of his welcome in the village when he returned from the service; saw how proud his father was before all the village of his Grigory, the moustached, stalwart soldier, so smart and handsome. Memory, the scourge of the unhappy, gives life to the very stones of the past and even into the poison drunk in old days pours drops of honey, so as to confound a man with his mistakes and, by making him love the past, rob him of hope for the future.

Tchelkash felt a rush of the softening, caressing air of home, bringing back to him the tender words of his mother and the weighty utterances of the venerable peasant, his father; many a forgotten sound and many a lush smell of mother-earth, freshly thawing, freshly ploughed, and freshly covered with the emerald silk of the corn. And he felt crushed, lost, pitiful, and solitary, torn up and cast out for ever from that life which had distilled the very blood that flowed in his veins.

"Hey! but where are we going?" Gavrilo asked suddenly.

Tchelkash started and looked round with the uneasy look of a bird of prey.

"Ah, the devil's taken the boat! No matter. Row a bit harder. We'll be there directly."

"You were dreaming?" Gavrilo enquired, smiling.

Tchelkash looked searchingly at him. The youth had completely regained his composure; he was calm, cheerful and even seemed somehow triumphant. He was very young, all his life lay before him. And he knew nothing. That was bad. Maybe the earth would keep hold of him. As these thoughts flashed through his head, Tchelkash felt still more mournful, and to Gavrilo he jerked out sullenly:

"I'm tired. And it rocks, too."

"It does rock, that's true. But now, I suppose, we shan't get caught with this?" Gavrilo shoved the bale with his foot.

"No. You can be easy. I shall hand it over directly and get the money. Oh, yes!"

"Five hundred?"

"Not less, I dare say."

"I say—that's a sum! If I, poor wretch, had that! Ah, I'd have a fine time with it."

"On your land?"

"To be sure! Why, I'd be off——"

And Gavrilo floated off into day dreams. Tchelkash seemed crushed. His moustaches drooped, his right side was soaked by the splashing of the waves, his eyes looked sunken and had lost their brightness. He was a pitiable and depressed figure. All that bird-of-prey look in his figure seemed somehow eclipsed under a humiliated moodiness, that showed itself in the very folds of his dirty shirt.

"I'm tired out, too—regularly done up."

"We'll be there directly. See over yonder."

Tchelkash turned the boat sharply, and steered it towards something black that stood up out of the water.

The sky was again all covered with clouds, and fine, warm rain had come on, pattering gaily on the crests of the waves.

"Stop! easy!" commanded Tchelkash.

The boat's nose knocked against the hull of the vessel.

"Are they asleep, the devils?" grumbled

Tchelkash, catching with his boat-hook on to some ropes that hung over the ship's side. "The ladder's not down. And this rain, too. As if it couldn't have come before! Hi, you spongeos. Hi! Hi!"

"Is that Selkash?" they heard a soft purring voice say overhead.

"Come, let down the ladder."

"Kalimera, Selkash."

"Let down the ladder, you smutty devil!" yelled Tchelkash.

"Ah, what a rage he's come in to-day. Ahoy!"

"Get up, Gavrilo!" Tchelkash said to his companion.

In a moment they were on the deck, where three dark bearded figures, eagerly chattering together, in a strange staccato tongue, looked over the side into Tchelkash's boat. The fourth, clad in a long gown, went up to him and pressed his hand without speaking, then looked suspiciously round at Gavrilo.

"Get the money ready for me by the morning," Tchelkash said to him shortly. "And now I'll go to sleep. Gavrilo, come along! Are you hungry?"

"I'm sleepy," answered Gavrilo, and five minutes later he was snoring in the dirty hold of the vessel, while Tchelkash, sitting beside him, tried on somebody's boots. Dreamily spitting on one side, he whistled angrily and mournfully between his teeth. Then he stretched himself out beside Gavrilo, and pulling the boots off his feet again and putting his arms under his head, he fell to gazing intently at the deck, and pulling his moustaches.

The vessel rocked softly on the frolicking water, there was a fretful creaking of wood somewhere, the rain pattered softly on the deck, and the waves splashed on the ship's side. Everything was melancholy and sounded like the lullaby of a mother, who has no hope of her child's happiness. And Tchelkash fell asleep.

III.

He was the first to wake, he looked round him uneasily, but at once regained his self-possession and stared at Gavrilo who was still asleep. He was sweetly snoring, and in his sleep smiled all over his childish sunburnt healthy face. Tchelkash sighed and climbed up the narrow rope-ladder. Through the port hole he saw a leaden strip of sky. It was daylight, but a dreary autumn greyness.

Tchelkash came back two hours later. His face was red, his moustaches were jauntily curled, a smile of good-humoured gaiety beamed on his lips. He was wearing a pair of stout high boots, a short jacket, and leather breeches, and he looked like a sportsman. His whole costume was worn, but strong, and very becoming to him, making him look broader, covering up his angularity, and giving him a military air.

"Hi, little calf, get up!" He gave Gavrilo a kick.

Gavrilo started up, and, not recognising him, stared at him in alarm with dull eyes. Tchelkash chuckled.

"Well, you do look—" Gavrilo brought out with a broad grin at last. "You're quite a gentleman!"

"We soon change. But, I say, you're easily scared! aye! How many times were you ready to die last night? eh? tell me!"

"Well, but just think, it's the first time I've ever been on such a job! Why one may lose one's soul for all one's life!"

"Well, would you go again? eh?"

"Again? Well—that—how can I say? For what inducement? that's the point!"

"Well, if it were for two rainbows?"

"Two hundred roubles, you mean? Well—I might."

"But, I say! what about your soul?"

"Oh, well—maybe one wouldn't lose it!" Gavrilo smiled. "One mightn't,—and it would make a man of one for all one's life."

Tchelkash laughed good-humouredly.

"All right! that's enough joking. Let's row to land. Get ready!"

"Why, I've nothing to do! I'm ready."

And soon they were in the boat again, Tchelkash at the rudder, Gavrilo at the oars. Above them the sky was grey, with clouds stretched evenly across it. The muddy green sea played with their boat, tossing it noisily on the waves that sportively flung bright salt drops into it. Far ahead from the boat's prow could be seen the yellow streak of the sandy shore, while from the stern there stretched away into the distance the free, gambolling sea, all furrowed over with racing flocks of billows, decked here and there with a narrow fringe of foam. Far away they could see numbers of vessels, rocking on the bosom of the sea, away on the left a whole forest of masts and the white fronts of the houses of the town. From that direction there floated across the sea a dull resounding roar, that mingled with the splash of the waves into a full rich music. And over all was flung a delicate veil of ash-coloured mist, that made things seem far from one another.

"Ah, there'll be a pretty dance by evening!" said Tchelkash, nodding his head at the sea.

"A storm?" queried Gavrilo, working vigorously at the waves with his oars. He was already wet through from head to foot with the splashing the wind blew on him from the sea.

"Aye, aye!" Tchelkash assented.

Gavrilo looked inquisitively at him, and his eyes expressed unmistakeable expectation of something.

"Well, how much did they give you?" he asked, at last, seeing that Tchelkash was not going to begin the conversation.

"Look!" said Tchelkash, holding out to

Gavrilo something he had pulled out of his pocket.

Gavrilo saw the rainbow-coloured notes and everything danced in brilliant rainbow tints before his eyes.

"I say! Why I thought you were bragging! That's—how much?"

"Five hundred and forty! A smart job!"

"Smart, yes!" muttered Gavrilo, with greedy eyes, watching the five hundred and forty roubles as they were put back again in his pocket. "Well, I never! What a lot of money!" and he sighed dejectedly.

"We'll have a jolly good spree, my lad!" Tchelkash cried, ecstatically. "Eh, we've enough to. Never fear, mate, I'll give you your share. I'll give you forty, eh? Satisfied? If you like, I'll give it you now!"

"If—you don't mind. Well? I wouldn't say no!"

Gavrilo was trembling all over with suspense and some other acute feeling that dragged at his heart.

"Ha—ha—ha! Oh, you devil's doll! 'I'd not say no!' Take it, mate, please! I beg you, indeed, take it! I don't know what to do with such a lot of money! You must help me out, take some, there!"

Tchelkash held out some red notes to Gavrilo. He took them with a shaking hand, let go the oars, and began stuffing them away in his bosom, greedily screwing up his eyes and drawing in his breath noisily, as though he had drunk something hot. Tchelkash watched him with an ironical smile. Gavrilo took up the oars again and rowed nervously, hurriedly, keeping his eyes down as though he were afraid of something. His shoulders and his ears were twitching.

"You're greedy. That's bad. But, of course, you're a peasant," Tchelkash said, musingly.

"But see what one can do with money!" cried Gavrilo, suddenly breaking into passionate excitement, and jerkily, hurriedly, as though chasing his thoughts and catching his words as they flew, he began to speak of life in the village with money and without money. Respect, plenty, independence, gladness!

Tchelkash heard him attentively, with a serious face and eyes filled with some dreamy thought. At times he smiled a smile of content.

"Here we are!" Tchelkash cried at last, interrupting Gavrilo.

A wave caught up the boat and neatly drove it on to the sand.

"Come, mate, now it's over. We must drag the boat up further, so that it shouldn't get washed away. They'll come and fetch it. Well, we must say good-bye! It's eight versts from here to the town. What are you going to do? Coming back to the town, eh?"

Tchelkash's face was radiant with a good-humouredly sly smile, and altogether he had the air of a man who had thought of something very pleasant for himself and a surprise to Gavrilo. Thrusting his hand into his pocket, he rustled the notes there.

"No—I—am not coming. I——" Gavrilo gasped, and seemed choking with something. Within him there was raging a whole storm of desires, of words, of feelings, that swallowed up one another and scorched him as with fire.

Tchelkash looked at him in perplexity.

"What's the matter with you?" he asked.

"Why——" But Gavrilo's face flushed, then turned gray, and he moved irresolutely, as though he were half longing to throw himself on Tchelkash, or half torn by some desire, the attainment of which was hard for him.

Tchelkash felt ill at ease at the sight of such excitement in this lad. He wondered what form it would take.

Gavrilo began laughing strangely, a laugh that was like a sob. His head was downcast, the expression of his face Tchelkash could not see; Gavrilo's ears only were dimly visible, and they turned red and then pale.

"Well, damn you!" Tchelkash waved his hand, "Have you fallen in love with me, or what? One might think you were a girl! Or is parting from me so upsetting? Hey, suckling! Tell me, what's wrong? or else I'm off!"

"You're going!!" Gavrilo cried aloud.

The sandy waste of the shore seemed to start at his cry, and the yellow ridges of sand washed by the sea-waves seemed quivering. Tchelkash started too. All at once Gavrilo tore himself from where he stood, flung himself at Tchelkash's feet, threw his arms round them, and drew them towards him. Tchelkash staggered; he sat heavily down on the sand, and grinding his teeth, brandished his long arm and clenched fist in the air. But before he had time to strike he was pulled up by Gavrilo's shame-faced and supplicating whisper:

"Friend! Give me—that money! Give it me, for Christ's sake! What is it to you? Why in one night—in only one night—while it would take me a year—Give it me—I will pray for you! Continually—in three churches—for the salvation of your soul! Why you'd cast it to the winds—while I'd put it into the land. O, give it me! Why, what does it mean to you? Did it cost you much? One night—and you're rich! Do a deed of mercy! You're a lost man, you see—you couldn't make your way—while I—oh, give it to me!"

Tchelkash, dismayed, amazed, and wrathful, sat on the sand, thrown backwards with his hands supporting him; he sat there in silence, rolling his eyes frightfully at the young peasant, who, ducking his head down at his knees, whispered his prayer to him in gasps. He shoved him away at last, jumped up to his feet, and thrusting his hands into his pockets, flung the rainbow notes at Gavrilo.

"There, cur! Swallow them!" he roared, shaking with excitement, with intense pity and hatred of this greedy slave. And as he flung him the money, he felt himself a hero. There was a reckless gleam in his eyes, an heroic air about his whole person.

"I'd meant to give you more, of myself. I felt sorry for you yesterday. I thought of the village. I thought: come, I'll help the lad. I was waiting to see what you'd do, whether you'd beg or not. While you!—Ah, you rag! you beggar! To be able—to torment oneself so—for money! You fool. Greedy devils! They're beside themselves—sell themselves for five copecks! eh?"

"Dear friend! Christ have mercy on you! Why, what have I now! thousands!! I'm a rich man!" Gavrilo shrilled in ecstasy, all trembling, as he stowed away the notes in his bosom. "Ah, you good man! Never will I forget you! Never! And my wife and my children—I'll bid them pray for you!"

Tchelkash listened to his shrieks and wails of ecstasy, looked at his radiant face that was contorted by greedy joy, and felt that he, thief and rake as he was, cast out from everything in life, would never be so covetous, so base, would never so forget himself. Never would he be like that! And this thought and feeling, filling him with a sense of his own independence and reckless daring, kept him beside Gavrilo on the desolate sea shore.

"You've made me happy!" shrieked Gavrilo, and snatching Tchelkash's hand, he pressed it to his face.

Tchelkash did not speak; he grinned like a wolf. Gavrilo still went on pouring out his heart:

"Do you know what I was thinking about? As we rowed here—I saw—the money—thinks I—I'll give it him—you—with the oar—one blow! the money's mine, and into the sea with him—you, that is—eh! Who'll miss him? said I. And if they do find him, they won't be inquisitive how—and who it was killed him. He's not a man, thinks I, that there'd be much fuss about! He's of no use in the world! Who'd stand up for him? No, indeed—eh?"

"Give the money here!" growled Tchelkash, clutching Gavrilo by the throat.

Gavrilo struggled away once, twice. Tchelkash's other arm twisted like a snake about him—there was the sound of a shirt tearing—and Gavrilo lay on the sand, with his eyes staring wildly, his fingers clutching at the air and his legs waving. Tchelkash, erect, frigid, rapacious-looking, grinned maliciously, laughed a broken, biting laugh, and his moustaches twitched nervously in his sharp angular face.

Never in all his life had he been so cruelly wounded, and never had he felt so vindictive.

"Well, are you happy now?" he asked Gavrilo through his laughter, and turning his back on him he walked away in the direction of the town. But he had hardly taken two steps when Gavrilo crouched like a cat on one knee, and with a wide sweep of his arm, flung a round stone at him, viciously, shouting:

"O—one!"

Tchelkash uttered a cry, clapped his hands to the nape of his neck, staggered forward, turned round to Gavrilo, and fell on his face on the sand. Gavrilo's heart failed him as he watched him. He saw him stir one leg, try to lift his head, and then stretch out, quivering like a bow-string. Then Gavrilo rushed fleeing away into the distance, where a shaggy black cloud hung over the foggy steppe, and it was dark. The waves whispered, racing up the sand, melting into it and racing back. The foam hissed and the spray floated in the air.

It began to rain, at first slightly, but soon a steady heavy downpour was falling in streams from the sky, weaving a regular network of fine threads of water, that at once hid the steppe and the sea. Gavrilo vanished behind it. For a long while nothing was to be seen, but the rain and the long figure of the man stretched on the sand by the sea. But suddenly Gavrilo ran back out of the rain. Like a bird he flew up to Tchelkash, dropped down beside him, and began to turn him over on the ground. His hand dipped into a warm, red stickiness. He shuddered and staggered back with a face pale and distraught.

"Brother, get up!" he whispered through the patter of the rain into Tchelkash's ear.

Revived by the water on his face, Tchelkash came to himself, and pushed Gavrilo away, saying, hoarsely:

"Get—away!"

"Brother! Forgive me—it was the devil tempted me," Gavrilo whispered, faltering, as he kissed Tchelkash's hand.

"Go along. Get away," he croaked.

"Take the sin from off my soul! Brother! Forgive me!"

"For—go away, do! Go to the devil!" Tchelkash screamed suddenly, and he sat up on the sand. His face was pale and angry, his eyes were glazed, and kept closing, as though he were very sleepy. "What more—do you want? You've done—your job—and go away! Be off!" And he tried to kick Gavrilo away, as he knelt, overwhelmed, beside him, but he could not, and would have rolled over again if Gavrilo had not held him up, putting his arms round his shoulders. Tchelkash's face was now on a level with Gavrilo's. Both were pale, piteous, and terrible-looking.

"Tfoo!" Tchelkash spat into the wide, open eyes of his companion.

Meekly Gavrilo wiped his face with his sleeve, and murmured:

"Do as you will. I won't say a word. For Christ's sake, forgive me!"

"Snivelling idiot! Even stealing's more than you can do!" Tchelkash cried scornfully, tearing a piece off his shirt under his jacket, and without a word, clenching his teeth now and then, he began binding up his head. "Did you take the notes?" he filtered through his teeth.

"I didn't touch them, brother! I didn't want them! there's ill-luck from them!"

Tchelkash thrust his hand into his jacket pocket, drew out a bundle of notes, put one rainbow-coloured note back in his pocket, and handed all the rest to Gavrilo.

"Take them and go!"

"I won't take them, brother. I can't! Forgive me!"

"T-take them, I say!" bellowed Tchelkash, glaring horribly.

"Forgive me! Then I'll take them," said Gavrilo, timidly, and he fell at Tchelkash's feet on the damp sand, that was being liberally drenched by the rain.

"You lie, you'll take them, sniveller!" Tchelkash said with conviction, and with an effort, pulling Gavrilo's head up by the hair, he thrust the notes in his face.

"Take them! take them! You didn't do your job for nothing, I suppose. Take it, don't be frightened! Don't be ashamed of having nearly killed a man! For people like me, no one will make much enquiry. They'll say thank you, indeed, when they know of it. There, take it! No one will ever know what you've done, and it deserves a reward. Come, now!"

Gavrilo saw that Tchelkash was laughing, and he felt relieved. He crushed the notes up tight in his hand.

"Brother! you forgive me? Won't you? eh?" he asked, tearfully.

"Brother of mine!" Tchelkash mimicked him as he got, reeling, on to his legs. "What for? There're nothing to forgive. To-day you do for me, to-morrow I'll do for you."

"Oh, brother, brother!" Gavrilo sighed mournfully, shaking his head.

Tchelkash stood facing him, he smiled strangely, and the rag on his head, growing gradually redder, began to look like a Turkish fez.

The rain streamed in bucketsful. The sea moaned wlth a hollow sound, and the waves beat on the shore, lashing furiously and wrathfully against it.

The two men were silent.

"Come, good-bye!" Tchelkash said, coldly and sarcastically.

He reeled, his legs shook, and he held his head queerly, as though he were afraid of losing it.

"Forgive me, brother!" Gavrilo besought him once more.

"All right!" Tchelkash answered, coldly, setting off on his way.

He walked away, staggering, and still holding

his head in his left hand, while he slowly tugged at his brown moustache with the right.

Gavrilo looked after him a long while, till he had disappeared in the rain, which still poured down in fine, countless streams, and wrapped everything in an impenetrable steel-gray mist.

Then Gavrilo took off his soaked cap, made the sign of the cross, looked at the notes crushed up in his hand, heaved a deep sigh of relief, thrust them into his bosom, and with long, firm strides went along the shore, in the opposite direction from that Tchelkash had taken.

The sea howled, flinging heavy, breaking billows on the sand of the shore, and dashing them into spray, the rain lashed the water and the earth, the wind blustered. All the air was full of roaring, howling, moaning. Neither distance nor sky could be seen through the rain.

Soon the rain and the spray had washed away the red patch on the spot where Tchelkash had lain, washed away the traces of Tchelkash and the peasant lad on the sandy beach. And no trace was left on the seashore of the little drama that had been played out between two men.

MY FELLOW-TRAVELLER.

(THE STORY OF A JOURNEY).

I MET him in the harbour of Odessa. For three successive days his square, strongly-built figure attracted my attention. His face—of a Caucasian type—was framed in a handsome beard. He haunted me. I saw him standing for hours together on the stone quay, with the handle of his walking stick in his mouth, staring down vacantly, with his black almond-shaped eyes, into the muddy waters of the harbour. Ten times a day, he would pass me by with the gait of a careless lounger. Whom could he be? I began to watch him. As if anxious to excite my curiosity, he seemed to cross my path more and more often. In the end, his fashionably-cut light check suit, his black hat, like that of an artist, his indolent lounge, and even his listless, bored glance grew quite familiar to me. His presence was utterly unaccountable, here in the harbour, where the whistling of the steamers and engines, the clanking of chains, the shouting of workmen, all the hurried maddening bustle of a port, dominated one's sensations, and deadened one's nerves and brain. Everyone else about the port was enmeshed in its immense complex machinery, which demanded incessant vigilance and endless toil. Everyone here was busy, loading and unloading either steamers or railway trucks. Everyone was tired and careworn. Everyone was hurrying to and fro, shouting or cursing, covered with dirt and sweat. In the midst of the toil and bustle this singular person, with his air of deadly boredom, strolled about deliberately, heedless of everything.

At last, on the fourth day, I came across him during the dinner hour, and I made up my mind to find out at any cost who he might be. I seated myself with my bread and water-melon not far from him, and began to eat, scrutinising him and devising some suitable pretext for beginning a conversation with him.

There he stood, leaning against a pile of tea-boxes, glancing aimlessly around, and drumming with his fingers on his walking stick, as if it were a flute. It was difficult for me, a man dressed like a tramp, with a porter's knot over my shoulders, and grimy with coal dust, to open up a conversation with such a dandy. But to my astonishment I noticed that he never took his eyes off me, and that an unpleasant, greedy, animal light shone in those eyes. I came to the conclusion that the object of my curiosity must be hungry, and after glancing rapidly round, I asked him in a low voice: "Are you hungry?"

He started, and with a famished grin showed rows of strong sound teeth. And he, too, looked suspiciously round. We were quite unobserved. Then I handed him half my melon and a chunk of wheaten bread. He snatched it all from my hand, and disappeared, squatting behind a pile of goods. His head peeped out from time to time; his hat was pushed back from his forehead, showing his dark moist brow. His face wore a broad smile, and for some unknown reason he kept winking at me, never for a moment ceasing to chew.

Making him a sign to wait a moment, I went away to buy meat, brought it, gave it to him, and stood by the boxes, thus completely shielding my poor dandy from outsiders' eyes. He was still eating ravenously, and constantly looking round as if afraid someone might snatch his food away; but after I returned, he began to eat more calmly, though still so fast and so greedily that it caused me pain to watch this famished man. And I turned my back on him.

"Thanks! Many thanks indeed!" He patted my shoulder, snatched my hand, pressed it, and shook it heartily.

Five minutes later he was telling me who he was. He was a Georgian prince, by name Shakro Ptadze, and was the only son of a rich landowner of Kutais in the Caucasus. He had held a position as clerk at one of the railway stations in his own country, and during that time had lived with a friend. But one fine day the friend disappeared, carrying off all the prince's money and valuables. Shakro determined to track and follow him, and having heard by chance that his late friend had taken a ticket to Batoum, he set off there. But in Batoum he found that his friend had gone on to Odessa. Then Prince Shakro borrowed a passport of another friend—a hair-dresser—of the same age as himself, though the features and distinguishing marks noted therein did not in the least resemble his own. Arrived at Odessa, he informed the police of his loss, and they promised to investigate the matter. He had been waiting for a fortnight, had consumed all his money, and for the last four days had not eaten a morsel.

I listened to his story, plentifully embellished as it was with oaths. He gave me the impression of being sincere. I looked at him, I believed him, and felt sorry for the lad. He was nothing more—he was nineteen, but from his naïvety one might have taken him for younger. Again and again, and with deep indignation, he returned to the thought of his close friendship for a man who had turned out to be a thief, and had stolen property of such value that Shakro's stern old father would certainly stab his son with a dagger if the property were not recovered.

I thought that if I didn't help this young fellow, the greedy town would suck him down. I knew through what trifling circumstances the army of tramps is recruited, and there seemed every possibility of Prince Shakro drifting into this respectable, but not respected class. I felt a wish to help him. My earnings were not sufficient to buy him a ticket to Batoum, so I visited some of the railway offices, and begged a free ticket for him. I produced weighty arguments in favour of assisting the young fellow, with the result of getting refusals just as weighty. I advised Shakro to apply to the Head of the Police of the town; this made him uneasy, and he declined to go there. Why not? He explained that he had not paid for his rooms at an hotel where he had been staying, and that when requested to do so, he had struck some one. This made him anxious to conceal his identity, for he supposed, and with reason, that if the police found him out he would have to account for the fact of his not paying his bill, and for having struck the man. Besides, he could not remember exactly if he had struck one or two blows, or more.

The position was growing more complicated.

I resolved to work till I had earned a sum sufficient to carry him back to Batoum. But alas! I soon realised that my plan could not be carried out quickly,—by no means quickly—for my half-starved prince ate as much as three men, and more. At that time there was a great influx of peasants into the Crimea from the famine-stricken northern parts of Russia, and this had caused a great reduction in the wages of the workers at the docks. I succeeded in earning only eighty kopecks a day, and our food cost us sixty kopecks.

I had no intention of staying much longer at Odessa, for I had meant, some time before I came across the prince, to go on to the Crimea. I therefore suggested to him the following plan: that we should travel together on foot to the Crimea, and there I would find him another companion, who would continue the journey with him as far as Tiflis; if I should fail in finding him a fellow-traveller, I promised to go with him myself.

The prince glanced sadly at his elegant boots, his hat, his trousers, whilst he smoothed and patted his coat. He thought a little time, sighed frequently, and at last agreed. So we started off from Odessa to Tiflis on foot.

II.

By the time we had arrived at Kherson I knew something of my companion. He was a naïvely savage, exceedingly undeveloped young fellow; gay when he was well fed, dejected when he was hungry, like a strong, easy-tempered animal. On the road he gave me accounts of life in the Caucasus, and told me much about the landowners; about their amusements, and the way they treated the peasantry. His stories were interesting, and had a beauty of their own; but they produced on my mind a most unfavourable impression of the narrator himself.

To give one instance. There was at one time a rich prince, who had invited many friends to a feast. They partook freely of all kinds of Caucasian wines and meats, and after the feast the prince led his guests to the stables. They saddled the horses, the prince picked out the handsomest, and rode him into the fields. That was a fiery steed! The guests praised his form and paces. Once more the prince started to ride round the field, when at the same moment a peasant appeared, riding a splendid white horse, and overtook the prince—overtook him and laughed proudly! The prince was put to shame before his guests! He knit his brow, and beckoned to the peasant to approach; then, with a blow of his dagger, he severed the man's head from his body. Drawing his pistol, he shot the white horse in the ear. He then delivered himself up to justice, and was condemned to penal servitude.

Through the whole story there rang a note of pity for the prince. I endeavoured to make Shakro understand that his pity was misplaced.

"There are not so many princes," he remarked didactically, "as there are peasants. It cannot be just to condemn a prince for a peasant. What, after all is a peasant? he is no better than this!" He took up a handful of soil, and added: "A prince is a star!"

We had a dispute over this question and he got angry. When angry, he showed his teeth like a wolf, and his features seemed to grow sharp and set.

"Maxime, you know nothing about life in the Caucasus; so you had better hold your tongue!" he shouted.

All my arguments were powerless to shatter his naïve convictions. What was clear to me seemed absurd to him. My arguments never reached his brain; but if ever I did succeed in showing him that my opinions were weightier and of more value than his own, he would simply say:

"Then go and live in the Caucasus, and you will see that I am right. What every one does *must* be right. Why am I to believe what you say? You are the only one who says such things are wrong; whilst thousands say they are right!"

Then I was silent, feeling that words were of no use in this case; only facts could confute a man, who believed that life, just as it is, is entirely just and lawful. I was silent, while he was triumphant, for he firmly believed that he knew life and considered his knowledge of it something unshakeable, stable and perfect. My silence seemed to him to give him a right to strike a fuller note in his stories of Caucasian life,—a life full of so much wild beauty, so much fire and originality. These stories, though full of interest and attraction for me, continued to provoke my indignation and disgust by their cruelty, by the worship of wealth and of strength which they displayed, and the absence of that morality which is said to be binding on all men alike.

Once I asked him if he knew what Christ had taught.

"Yes, of course I do!" he replied, shrugging his shoulders.

But after I had examined him on this point, it turned out that all he knew was, that there had once been a certain Christ, who protested against the laws of the Jews, and that for this protest he was crucified by the Jews. But being a God, he did not die on the cross, but ascended into heaven, and gave the world a new law.

"What law was that?" I inquired.

He glanced at me with ironical incredulity, and asked: "Are you a Christian? Well, so am I a Christian. Nearly all the people in the world are Christians. Well, why do you ask then? You know the way they all live; they follow the law of Christ!"

I grew excited, and began eagerly to tell him about Christ's life. At first he listened attentively; but this attention did not last long, and he began to yawn.

I understood that it was useless appealing to his heart, and I once more addressed myself to his head, and talked to him of the advantages of mutual help and of knowledge, the benefits of obedience to the law, speaking of the policy of morality and nothing more.

"He who is strong is a law to himself! He has no need of learning; even blind, he'll find his way," Prince Shakro replied, languidly.

Yes, he was always true to himself. This made me feel a respect for him; but he was savage and cruel, and sometimes I felt a spark of hatred for Prince Shakro. Still, I had not lost all hope of finding some point of contact with him, some common ground on which we could meet, and understand one another.

I began to use simpler language with the prince, and tried to put myself mentally on a level with him. He noticed these attempts of mine, but evidently mistaking them for an acknowledgement on my part of his superiority, adopted a still more patronising tone in talking to me. I suffered, as the conviction came home to me, that all my arguments were shattered against the stone wall of his conception of life.

III.

Soon we had left Perekop behind us. We were approaching the Crimean mountains. For the last two days we had seen them against the horizon. The mountains were pale blue, and looked like soft heaps of billowy clouds. I admired them in the distance, and I dreamed of the southern shore of the Crimea. The prince hummed his Georgian songs and was gloomy. We had spent all our money,and there was no chance of earning anything in these parts.

We bent our steps towards Feodosia, where a new harbour was in course of construction. The prince said that he would work, too, and that when we had earned enough money we would take a boat together to Batoum. In Batoum, he said, he had many friends, and with their assistance he could easily get me a situation—as a house-porter or a watchman. He clapped me patronisingly on the back, and remarked, indulgently, with a peculiar click of his tongue:

"I'll arrange it for you! You shall have such a life! tsé, tsé! You will have plenty of wine, there will be as much mutton as you can eat. You can marry a fat Georgian girl; tsé, tsé, tsé! She will cook you Georgian dishes; give you children—many, many children! tsé, tsé, tsé!"

This constant repetition of "tsé, tsé, tsé!"

surprised me at first; then it began to irritate me, and, at last, it reduced me to a melancholy frenzy. In Russia we use this sound to call pigs, but in the Caucasus it seems to be an expression of delight and of regret, of pleasure and of sadness.

Shakro's smart suit already began to look shabby; his elegant boots had split in many places. His cane and hat had been sold in Kherson. To replace the hat he had bought an old uniform cap of a railway clerk. When he put this cap on for the first time, he cocked it on one side of his head, and asked: "Does it suit me? Do I look nice?"

IV.

At last we reached the Crimea. We had left Simpheropol behind us, and were moving towards Jalta.

I was walking along in silent ecstasy, marvelling at the beauty of this strip of land, caressed on all sides by the sea.

The prince sighed, complained, and, casting dejected glances about him, tried filling his empty stomach with wild berries. His knowledge of their nutritive qualities was extremely limited, and his experiments were not always successful. Often he would remark, ill-humouredly:

"If I'm turned inside out with eating this stuff, how am I to go any further? And what's to be done then?"

We had no chance of earning anything, neither had we a penny left to buy a bit of bread, All we had to live on was fruit, and our hopes for the future.

The prince began to reproach me with want of enterprise and laziness—with "gaping about," as he expressed it. Altogether, he was beginning to bore me; but what most tried my patience were his fabulous accounts of his appetite. According to these accounts, after a hearty breakfast at noon of roast lamb, and three bottles of wine, he could easily, at his two o'clock dinner, dispose of three plates of soup, a pot of pilave, a dish of shasleek, and various other Caucasian dishes, washed down abundantly with wine. For whole days he would talk of nothing but his gastronomic tastes and knowledge: and whilst thus talking, he would smack his lips, his eyes would glow, he would show his teeth, and grind them together; would suck in and swallow the saliva that came dripping from his eloquent lips. Watching him at these moments, I conceived for him a deep feeling of disgust, which I found difficult to conceal.

Near Jalta I obtained a job at clearing away the dead branches in an orchard. I was paid fifty kopecks in advance, and laid out the whole of this money on bread and meat. No sooner had I returned with my purchase, than the gardener called me away to my work. I had to leave my store of food with Shakro, who, under the pretext of a headache, had declined to work. When I returned in an hour's time, I had to acknowledge that Shakro's stories of his appetite were all too true. Not a crumb was left of all the food I had bought! His action was anything but a friendly one, but I let it pass. Later on I had to acknowledge to myself the mistake I then made.

My silence did not pass unnoticed by Shakro, who profited by it in his own fashion. His behaviour towards me from that time grew more and more shameless. I worked, while he ate and drank and urged me on, refusing, on various pretexts, to do any work himself. I am no follower of Tolstoi. I felt amused and sad as I saw this strong healthy lad watching me with greedy eyes when I returned from a hard day's labour, and found him waiting for me in some shady nook. But it was even more mortifying to see that he was sneering at me for working. He sneered at me because he had learnt to beg, and because he looked on me as a lifeless dummy. When he first started begging, he was ashamed for me to see him, but he soon got over this; and as soon as we came to some Tartar village, he would openly prepare for business. Leaning heavily on his stick, he would drag one foot after him, as though he were lame. He knew quite well that the Tartars were mean, and never give alms to anyone who is strong and well. I argued with him, and tried to convince him of the shamefulness of such a course of action. He only sneered.

"I cannot work," was all he would reply.

He did not get much by his begging.

My health at that time began to give way. Every day the journey seemed to grow more trying. Every day our relations towards each other grew more strained. Shakro, now, had begun shamelessly to insist that I should provide him with food.

"It was you," he would say, "who brought me out here, all this way; so you must look after me. I never walked so far in my life before. I should never have undertaken such a journey on foot. It may kill me! You are tormenting me; you are crushing the life out of me! Think what it would be if I were to die! My mother would weep; my father would weep; all my friends would weep! Just think of all the tears that would be shed!"

I listened to such speeches, but was not angered by them. A strange thought began to stir in my mind, a thought that made me bear with him patiently. Many a time as he lay asleep by my side I would watch his calm, quiet face, and think to myself, as though groping after some idea:

"He is my fellow-traveller—my fellow-traveller."

At times, a dim thought would strike me, that after all Shakro was only right in claiming so freely, and with so much assurance, my help and my care. It proved that he possessed a strong will. He was enslaving me, and I submitted, and studied his character, following each quivering movement of the muscles of his face, trying to foresee when and at what point he would stop in this process of exploiting another person's individuality.

Shakro was in excellent spirits; he sang, and slept, and jeered at me, when he felt so disposed. Sometimes we separated for two or three days. I would leave him some bread and some money (if we had any), and would tell him where to meet me again. At parting, he would follow me with a suspicious, angry look in his eyes. But when we met again he welcomed me with gleeful triumph. He always said, laughing: "I thought you had run off alone, and left me! ha! ha! ha!" I brought him food, and told him of the beautiful places I had seen; and once even, speaking of Bakhtchesarai, I told him about our Russian poet Pushkin, and recited some of his verses. But this produced no effect on him.

"Oh, indeed; that is poetry, is it? Well, songs are better than poetry. I knew a Georgian once! *He* was the man to sing! He sang so loud—so loud—one would have thought his throat was being cut? He finished by murdering an inn-keeper, and was banished to Siberia."

Every time I returned, I sank lower and lower in the opinion of Shakro, until he could not conceal his contempt for me. Our position was anything but pleasant. I was seldom lucky enough to earn more than a rouble or a rouble and a-half a week, and I need not say that was not nearly sufficient to feed us both. The few bits of money that Shakro gained by begging made but little difference in the state of our affairs, for his belly was as a bottomless pit, which swallowed everything that fell in its way; grapes, melons, salt fish, bread, or dried fruit; and as time went on he seemed to need ever more and more food.

Shakro began to urge me to hasten our departure from the Crimea, not unreasonably pointing out that autumn would soon be here and we had a long way still to go. I agreed with this view, and, besides, I had by then seen all that part of the Crimea. So we pushed on again towards Feodosia, hoping to earn something there. Once more our diet was reduced to fruit, and to hopes for the future.

Poor future! Such a load of hopes is cast on

it by men, that it loses almost all its charm by the time it becomes the present!

When within some twenty versts of Aloushta we stopped, as usual, for our night's rest. I had persuaded Shakro to keep to the sea coast; it was a longer way round, but I longed to breathe the fresh sea breezes. We made a fire, and lay down beside it. The night was a glorious one. The dark green sea splashed against the rocks below; above us spread the majestic calm of the blue heavens, and around us sweet-scented trees and bushes rustled softly. The moon was rising, and the delicate tracery of the shadows, thrown by the tall, green plane trees, crept over the stones. Somewhere near a bird sang; its note was clear and bold. Its silvery trill seemed to melt into the air that was full of the soft, caressing splash of the waves. The silence that followed was broken by the nervous chirp of a cricket. The fire burnt bright, and its flames looked like a large bunch of red and yellow flowers. Flickering shadows danced gaily around us, as if exulting in their power of movement, in contrast with the creeping advance of the moon shadows. From time to time strange sounds floated through the air. The broad expanse of sea horizon seemed lost in immensity. In the sky overhead not a cloud was visible. I felt as if I were lying on the earth's extreme edge, gazing into infinite space, that riddle that haunts the soul. The majestic beauty of the night intoxicated me, whilst my whole being seemed absorbed in the harmony of its colours, its sounds, and its scents.

A feeling of awe filled my soul, a feeling as if something great were very near to me. My heart throbbed with the joy of life.

Suddenly, Shakro burst into loud laughter "Ha! ha! ha! How stupid your face does look! You've a regular sheep's head! Ha! ha! ha!

I started as though it were a sudden clap of thunder. But it was worse. It was laughable, yes, but oh, how mortifying it was!

He, Shakro, laughed till the tears came. I was ready to cry, too, but from quite a different reason. A lump rose in my throat, and I could not speak. I gazed at him with wild eyes, and this only increased his mirth. He rolled on the ground, holding his sides. As for me, I could not get over the insult—for a bitter insult it was. Those—few, I hope—who will understand it, from having had a similar experience in their lives, will recall all the bitterness it left in their souls.

"Leave off!" I shouted, furiously.

He was startled and frightened, but he could not at once restrain his laughter. His eyes rolled, and his cheeks swelled as if about to burst. All at once he went off into a guffaw again. Then I rose and left him.

For some time I wandered about, heedless and almost unconscious of all that surrounded me, my whole soul consumed with the bitter pang of loneliness and of humiliation. Mentally, I had been embracing all nature. Silently, with the passionate love any man must feel if he has a little of the poet in him, I was loving and adoring her. And now it was nature that, under the form of Shakro, was mocking me for my passion. I might have gone still further in my accusations against nature, against Shakro, and against the whole of life, had I not been stopped by approaching footsteps.

"Do not be angry," said Shakro in a contrite voice, touching my shoulder lightly. "Were you praying? I didn't know it, for I never pray myself."

He spoke timidly, like a naughty child. In

spite of my excitement, I could not help noticing his pitiful face, ludicrously distorted by embarrassment and alarm.

"I will never interfere with you again. Truly! Never!" He shook his head emphatically. "I know you are a quiet fellow. You work hard, and do not force me to do the same. I used to wonder why: but, of course, it's because you are foolish as a sheep!"

That was his way of consoling me! That was his idea of asking forgiveness! After such consolation, and such excuses, what was there left for me to do but forgive, not only for the past, but for the future?

Half an hour later he was sound asleep, whilst I sat beside him, watching him. During sleep, every one, be he ever so strong, looks helpless and weak, but Shakro looked a pitiful creature. His thick, half-parted lips, and his arched eyebrows, gave to his face a childish look of timidity and of wonder. His breathing was quiet and regular, though at times he moved restlessly, and muttered rapidly in the Georgian language: the words seemed those of entreaty. All around us reigned that intense calm, which always makes one somehow expectant, and which, were it to last long, might drive one mad by its absolute stillness and the absence of sound—the vivid shadow of motion, for sound and motion seem ever allied.

The soft splash of the waves did not reach us. We were resting in a hollow gorge that was overgrown with bushes, and looked like the shaggy mouth of some petrified monster. I still watched Shakro, and thought: "This is my fellow traveller. I might leave him here, but I could never get away from him, or the like of him; their name is legion. This is my life companion. He will leave me only at death's door."

V.

At Feodosia we were sorely disappointed. All the work there was already apportioned among Turks, Greeks, Georgians, tramps, and Russian peasants from Poltava and Smolensk, who had all arrived before us. Already, more than four hundred men had, like ourselves, come in the hopes of finding employment; and were also, like ourselves, destined to remain silent spectators of the busy work going on in the port. In the town, and outside also, we met groups of famished peasants, grey and careworn, wandering miserably about. Of tramps there were also plenty, roving around like hungry wolves.

At first these tramps took us for famished peasants, and tried to make what they could out of us. They tore from Shakro's back the overcoat which I had bought him, and they snatched my knapsack from my shoulders. After several discussions, they recognised our intellectual and social kinship with them; and they returned us all our belongings. Tramps are men of honour, though they may be great rogues.

Seeing that there was no work for us, and that the construction of the harbour was going on very well without our help, we moved on resentfully towards Kertch.

My friend kept his word, and never again molested me; but he was terribly famished, his countenance was as black as thunder. He ground his teeth together, as does a wolf, whenever he saw someone else eating; and he terrified me by the marvellous accounts of the quantity of food he was prepared to consume. Of late he had begun to talk about women, at first only casually, with sighs of regret. But by degrees he came to talk more and more often on the subject, with the lascivious smile of "an Oriental." At length his state became such, that he could not see any person of the other sex, whatever her age or appearance, without letting fall some obscene remark about her looks or her figure. He spoke of women so freely, with so wide a knowledge of the sex; and his point of view, when discussing women, was so astoundingly direct, that his conversation filled me with disgust. Once I tried to prove to him that a woman was a being in no way inferior to him. I saw that he was not merely mortified by my words, but was on the point of violently resenting them as a personal insult. So I postponed my arguments till such time as Shakro should be well fed once more.

In order to shorten our road to Kertch we left the coast, and tramped across the steppes. There was nothing in my knapsack but a three-pound loaf of barley bread, which we had bought of a Tartar with our last five-kopeck piece. Owing to this painful circumstance, when, at last we reached Kertch, we could hardly move our legs, so seeking therefore work was out of the question. Shakro's attempts to beg by the way had proved unsuccessful; everywhere he had received the curt refusal: "There are so many of you."

This was only too true, for the number of people, who, during that bitter year, were in want of bread, was appalling. The famished peasants roamed about the country in groups, from three to twenty or more together. Some carried babies in their arms; some had young children dragging by the hand. The children looked almost transparent, with a bluish skin, under which flowed, instead of pure blood, some sort of thick unwholesome fluid. The way their small sharp bones projected from under the wasted flesh spoke more eloquently than could any words. The sight of them made one's heart ache, whilst a constant intolerable pain seemed to gnaw one's very soul.

These hungry, naked, worn-out children did not even cry. But they looked about them with sharp eyes that flashed greedily whenever they saw a garden, or a field, from which the corn had not yet been carried. Then they would glance sadly at their elders, as if asking "Why was I brought into this world?"

Sometimes they had a cart, driven by a dried-up skeleton of an old woman, and full of children, whose little heads peeped out, gazing with mournful eyes in expressive silence at the new land into which they had been brought. The rough, bony horse dragged itself along, shaking its head and its tumbled mane wearily from side to side.

Following the cart, or clustering round it, came the grown-up people, with heads sunk low on their breasts, and arms hanging helplessly at their sides. Their dim, vacant eyes had not even the feverish glitter of hunger, but were full of an indescribable, impressive mournfulness. Cast out of their homes by misfortune, these processions of peasants moved silently, slowly, stealthily through the strange land, as if afraid that their presence might disturb the peace of the more fortunate inhabitants. Many and many a time we came across these processions, and every time they reminded me of a funeral without the corpse.

Sometimes, when they overtook us, or when we passed them, they would timidly and quietly ask us: "Is it much further to the village?" And when we answered, they would sigh, and gaze dumbly at us. My travelling companion hated these irrepressible rivals for charity.

In spite of all the difficulties of the journey, and the scantiness of our food, Shakro, with his rich vitality, could not acquire the lean, hungry look, of which the starving peasants could boast in its fullest perfection. Whenever he caught sight, in the distance, of these latter, he would exclaim: "Pouh! pouh! pouh! Here they are again! What are they roaming about for? They seem to be always on the move! Is Russia too small for them? I can't understand what they want! Russians are a stupid sort of people!"

When I had explained to him the reason of the "stupid" Russians coming to the Crimea, he shook his head incredulously, and remarked: "I don't understand! It's nonsense! We never have such 'stupid' things happening in Georgia!"

We arrived in Kertch, as I have said, exhausted and hungry. It was late. We had to spend the night under a bridge, which joined the harbour to the mainland. We thought it better to conceal ourselves, as we had been told that just before our arrival all the tramps had been driven out of the town. This made us feel anxious, lest we might fall into the hands of the police; besides Shakro had only a false passport, and if that fact became known, it might lead to serious complications in our future.

All night long the spray from the sea splashed over us. At dawn we left our hiding place, wet to the skin and bitterly cold. All day we wandered about the shore. All we succeeded in earning was a silver piece of the value of ten kopecks, which was given me by the wife of a priest, in return for helping her to carry home a bag of melons from the bazaar.

A narrow belt of water divided us from Taman, where we meant to go, but not one boatman would consent to carry us over in his boat, in spite of my pleadings. Everyone here was up in arms against the tramps, who, shortly before our arrival, had performed a series of heroic exploits; and we were looked upon, with good reason, as belonging to their set.

Evening came on. I felt angry with the whole world, for my lack of success; and I planned a somewhat risky scheme, which I put into execution as soon as night came on.

VI.

Towards evening, Shakro and I stole quietly up towards the boats of the custom-house guard-ship. There were three of them, chained to iron rings, which rings were firmly screwed into the stone wall of the quay. It was pitch dark. A strong wind dashed the boats one against the other. The iron chains clanked noisily. In the darkness and the noise, it was easy for me to unscrew the ring from the stone wall.

Just above our heads the sentinel walked to and fro, whistling through his teeth a tune. Whenever he approached I stopped my work, though, as a matter of fact, this was a useless precaution; he could not even have suspected that a person would sit up to his neck in the water, at a spot where the back-wash of a wave might at any moment carry him off his feet. Besides, the chains never ceased clanking, as the wind swung them backwards and forwards. Shakro was already lying full-length along the bottom of the boat, muttering something, which the noise of the waves prevented me from hearing. At last the ring was in my hand. At the same moment a wave caught our boat, and dashed it suddenly some ten yards away from the side of the quay. I had to swim for a few seconds by the side of the boat, holding the chain in my hand. At last I managed to scramble in. We tore up two boards from the bottom, and using these as oars, I paddled away as fast as I could.

Clouds sailed rapidly over our heads; around, and underneath the boat, waves splashed furiously. Shakro sat aft. Every now and then I lost sight of him as the whole stern of the boat slipped into some deep watery gulf; the next moment he would rise high above my head, shouting desperately, and almost falling forwards into my arms. I told him not to shout, but to fasten his feet to the seat of the boat, as I had already fastened mine. I feared his shouts might give the alarm. He obeyed, and grew so silent that I only knew he was in the boat by the white spot opposite to me, which I knew must be his face. The whole time he held the rudder in his hand; we could not change places, we dared not move.

From time to time I called out instructions as to the handling of the boat, and he understood me so quickly, and did everything so cleverly, that one might have thought he had been born a sailor. The boards I was using in the place of oars were of little use; they only blistered my hands. The furious gusts of wind served to carry the boat forward. I cared little for the direction, my only thought was to get the boat across to the other side. It was not difficult to steer, for the lights in Kertch were still visible, and served as a beacon. The waves splashed over our boat with angry hissings. The further across we got, the more furious and the wilder became the waves. Already we could hear a sort of roar that held mind and soul as with a spell. Faster and faster our boat flew on before the wind, till it became almost impossible to steer a course. Every now and then we would sink into a gulf, and the next moment we would rise high on the summit of some enormous watery hill. The darkness was increasing, the clouds were sinking lower and lower. The lights of the town had disappeared.

Our state was growing desperate. It seemed as if the expanse of angry rollers was boundless and limitless. We could see nothing but these immense waves, that came rolling, one after another, out of the gloom, straight on to our boat. With an angry crash a board was torn from my hand, forcing me to throw the other into the boat, and to hold on tight with both hands to the gunwale. Every time the boat was thrown upwards, Shakro shrieked wildly. As for me, I felt wretched and helpless, in the darkness, surrounded with angry waves, whose noise deafened me. I stared about me in dull and chilly terror, and saw the awful monotony around us. Waves, nothing but waves, with whitish crests, that broke in showers of salt spray; above us, the thick ragged-edged clouds were like waves too.

I became conscious only of one thing: I felt that all that was going on around me might be immeasurably more majestic and more terrible, but that it did not deign to be, and was restraining its strength; and that I resented. Death is inevitable. But that impartial law, reducing all to the same commonplace level, seems to need something beautiful to compensate for its coarseness and cruelty. If I were asked to choose between a death by burning, or being suffocated in a dirty bog, I should choose the former; it is any way, a more seemly death.

"Let us rig up a sail," exclaimed Shakro.

"Where am I to find one?"

"Use my overcoat."

"Chuck it over to me then; but mind you don't drop the rudder into the water!"

Shakro quietly threw it over to me. "Here! Catch hold!"

Crawling along the bottom of the boat, I succeeded in pulling up another board, one end of which I fixed into one of the sleeves of the coat. I then fixed the board against the seat, and held it there with my feet. I was just going to take hold of the other sleeve, when an unexpected thing happened. The boat was tossed suddenly upwards, and then overturned. I felt myself in the water, holding the overcoat in one hand, and a rope, that was fastened to the boat, in the other hand. The waves swirled noisily over my head, and I swallowed a mouthful of bitter salt water. My nose, my mouth, and my ears, were full of it.

With all my might I clutched the rope, as the waves threw me backwards and forwards. Several times I sank, each time, as I rose again, bumping my head against the sides of the boat.

At last I succeeded in throwing the coat over the bottom of the boat, and tried to clamber on it myself. After a dozen efforts I scrambled up and I sat astride it. Then I caught sight of Shakro in the water on the opposite side of the boat, holding with both hands to the same rope of which I had just let go. The boat was apparently encircled by a rope, threaded through iron rings, driven into the outer planks.

"Alive!" I shouted.

At that moment Shakro was flung high up into the air, and he, too, got on to the boat. I clutched him, and there we remained sitting face to face, astride on the capsized boat! I sat on it as though it were a horse, making use of the rope as if it had been stirrups; but our position there was anything but safe—a wave might easily have knocked us out of our saddle. Shakro held tightly by my knees, and dropped his head on my breast. He shivered, and I could hear his teeth chattering. Something had to be done. The bottom of the upturned boat was slippery, as though it it had been greased with butter. I told Shakro to get into the water again, and hold by the ropes on one side of the boat, while I would do the same on the other side.

By way of reply, Shakro began to butt his head violently against my chest. The waves swept, in their wild dance, every now and then over us. We could hardly hold on our seats; the rope was cutting my leg desperately. As far as one could see there was nothing but immense waves, rising mountains high, only to disappear again noisily.

I repeated my advice to Shakro in a tone of command. He fell to butting me more violently than ever. There was no time to be lost. Slowly and with difficulty I tore his hands from me, and began to push him into the water, trying to make his hands take hold of the rope. Then something happened that dismayed me more than anything in that terrible night.

"Are you drowning me?" he muttered, gazing at me.

This was really horrible! The question itself was a dreadful one, but the tone in which it was uttered was more so. In it there was a timid submission to fate, and an entreaty for mercy, and the last sigh of one who had lost all hope of escaping from a frightful death. But more terrible still were the eyes that stared at me out of the wet, livid, death-like face.

"Hold on tighter!" I shouted to him, at the same time getting into the water myself, and taking hold of the rope. As I did so, I struck my foot against something, and for a moment I could not think for the pain. Then I understood. Suddenly a burning thought flashed through my mind. I felt delirious and stronger than ever.

"Land!" I shouted.

Great explorers may have shouted the word with more feeling on discovering new lands, but I doubt if any can have shouted more loudly. Shakro howled with delight, and we both rushed on in the water. But soon we both lost heart, for we were up to our chests in the waves, and still there seemed no sign of dry land. The waves were neither so strong nor so high, but they rolled slowly over our heads. Fortunately I had not let go of the boat, but still held on by the rope, which had already helped us when struggling in the water. Shakro and I moved carefully forward, towing the boat, which we had now righted, behind us.

Shakro was muttering and laughing. I glanced anxiously around. It was still dark. Behind us, and to our right, the roaring of the waves seemed to be increasing, whereas to our left and in front of us it was evidently growing less. We moved towards the left. The bottom was hard and sandy, but full of holes; sometimes we could not touch the bottom, and we had to take hold of the boat with one hand, while with the other hand, and our legs, we propelled it forward. At times again the water was no higher than our knees. When we came to the deep places Shakro howled, and I trembled with fear. Suddenly we saw ahead of us a light—we were safe!

Shakro shouted with all his might, but I could not forget that the boat was not ours, and promptly reminded him of the fact. He was silent, but a few minutes later I heard him sobbing. I could not quiet him—it was hopeless. But the water was gradually growing shallower, it reached our knees, then our ankles; and at last we felt dry land! We had dragged the boat so far, but our strength failed us, and we left it. A black log of wood lay across our path; we jumped over it, and stepped with our bare feet on to some prickly grass. It seemed unkind of the land to give us such a cruel welcome, but we did not heed it, and ran towards the fire. It was about a mile away; but it shone cheerily through the hovering gloom of the night, and seemed to smile a welcome to us.

VII.

Three enormous shaggy dogs leaped up out of the darkness and ran towards us. Shakro, who had been sobbing all the way, now shrieked, and threw himself on the ground. I flung the wet overcoat at the dogs, and stooped down to find a stick or a stone. I could feel nothing but coarse, prickly grass, which hurt my hands. The dogs continued their attack. I put my fingers into my mouth, and whistled as loud as I could. They rushed back, and at the same time we heard the sound of approaching steps and voices.

A few minutes later, and we were comfortably seated round a fire in the company of four shepherds, dressed in "touloups" or long sheepskin overcoats.

They scrutinised us keenly and rather suspiciously, and remained silent all the time I was telling them our story.

Two of the shepherds were seated on the ground, smoking, and puffing from their mouths clouds of smoke. The third was a tall man with a thick black beard, wearing a high fur cap. He stood behind us, leaning on a huge knotted stick. The fourth man was younger, and fair haired; he was helping the sobbing Shakro to get off his wet clothes. An enormous stick, the size of which alone inspired fear, lay beside each of the seated shepherds.

Ten yards away from us all the steppe seemed covered with something grey and undulating, which had the appearance of snow in spring time, just when it is beginning to thaw. It was only after a close inspection that one could discern that this grey waving mass was composed of many thousands of sheep, huddled closely together, asleep, forming in the dark night one compact mass. Sometimes they bleated piteously and timidly.

I dried the overcoat by the fire, and told the shepherds all our story truthfully; even describing the way in which we became possessed of the boat.

"Where is that boat now?" enquired the severe-looking elder man, who kept his eyes fixed on me.

I told him.

"Go, Michael, and look for it."

Michael, the shepherd with the black beard, went off with his stick over his shoulder, towards the sea-shore.

The overcoat was dry. Shakro was about to put it on his naked body, when the old man said: "Go and have a run first to warm yourself. Run quickly round the fire. Come!"

At first, Skakro did not understand. Then suddenly he rose from his place, and began dancing some wild dance of his own, first flying like a ball across the fire, then whirling round and round in one place, then stamping his feet on the ground, whilst he swung his arms, and shouted at the top of his voice. It was a ludicrous spectacle. Two of the shepherds were rolling on the ground, convulsed with laughter, while the older man, with a serious, immovable face, tried to clap his hands in time to the dancing, but could not succeed in doing so. He watched attentively every movement of the dancing Shakro, whilst he nodded his head, and exclaimed in a deep bass voice:

"Hè! Hè! That's right! Hè! Hè!"

The light fell full on Shakro, showing the variety of his movements, as at one moment he would coil himself up like a snake, and the next would dance round on one leg; then would plunge into a succession of rapid steps, difficult to follow with the eye. His naked body shone in the fire light, whilst the large beads of sweat, as they rolled off it, looked, in the red light of the fire, like drops of blood.

By now, all three of the shepherds were clapping their hands; whilst I, shivering with cold, dried myself by the fire, and thought that our adventures would gratify the taste of admirers of Cooper or of Jules Verne; there was shipwreck, then came hospitable aborigines, and a savage dance round the fire. And while I reflected thus, I felt very uneasy as to the chief point in every adventure—the end of it.

When Shakro had finished dancing, he also sat down by the fire, wrapped up in the overcoat. He was already eating, whilst he stared at me with his black eyes, which had a gleam in them of something I did not like. His clothes, stretched on sticks, driven into the ground, were drying before the fire. The shepherds had given me, also, some bread and bacon.

Michael returned, and sat down without a word beside the old man, who remarked in an enquiring voice: "Well?"

"I have found the boat," was the brief reply.

"It won't be washed away?"

"No."

The shepherds were silent, once more scrutinising us.

"Well," said Michael, at last, addressing no one in particular. "Shall we take them to the Ataman, or straight to the custom-house officers?"

"So that's to be the end!" I thought to myself.

Nobody replied to Michael's question. Shakro went on quietly with his eating, and said nothing.

"We could take them to the Ataman—or we could take them to the custom house. One plan's as good as the other," remarked the old man, after a short silence.

"They have stolen the custom house boat, so they ought to be taught a lesson for the future."

"Wait a bit, old man," I began.

"Certainly, they ought not to have stolen the boat. If they are not punished now, they will probably do something worse next time." The old man interrupted me, without paying any heed to my protestations.

The old man spoke with revolting indifference. When he had finished speaking, his comrades nodded their heads in token of assent.

"Yes, if a man steals, he has to bear the consequences, when he's caught— Michael! what about the boat? Is it there?"

"Oh, it's there all right!"

"Are you sure the waves won't wash it away?"

"Quite sure."

"Well, that's all right. Then let it stay there. To-morrow the boatmen will be going over to Kertch, and they can take it with them. They will not mind taking an empty boat along with them, will they? Well,—so you mean to say you were not frightened, you vagabonds! Weren't you indeed? La! la! la! Half a mile further out, and you would have been by this time at the bottom of the sea! What would you have done if the waves had cast you back into the sea? Ay, sure enough, you would have sunk to the bottom like a couple of axes. And that would have been the end of you both!"

As the old man finished speaking, he looked at me with an ironical smile on his lips.

"Well, why don't you speak, lad?" he enquired.

I was vexed by his reflections, which I misinterpreted as sneering at us. So I only answered rather sharply:

"I was listening to you."

"Well,—and what do you say?" enquired the old man.

"Nothing."

"Why are you rude to me? Is it the right thing to be rude to a man older than yourself?"

I was silent, acknowledging in my heart that it really was not the right thing.

"Won't you have something more to eat?" continued the old shepherd.

"No, I can't eat any more."

"Well, don't have any, if you don't want it. Perhaps you'll take a bit of bread with you to eat on the road?"

I trembled with joy, but would not betray my feelings.

"Oh, yes. I should like to take some with me for the road," I answered, quietly.

"I say, lads! give these fellows some bread and a piece of bacon each. If you can find something else, give it to them too."

"Are we to let them go, then?" asked Michael.

The other two shepherds looked up at the old man.

"What can they do here?"

"Did we not intend to take them either to the Ataman or to the custom house?" asked Michael, in a disappointed tone.

Shakro stirred uneasily in his seat near the fire, and poked out his head enquiringly from beneath the overcoat. He was quite serene.

"What would they do at the Ataman's? I should think there is nothing to do there just now. Perhaps later on they might like to go there?"

"But how about the boat?" insisted Michael.

"What about the boat?" enquired the old man again. "Did you not say the boat was all right where it was?"

"Yes, it's all right there," Michael replied.

"Well, let it stay there. In the morning John can row it round into the harbour. From there, someone will get it over to Kertch. That's all we can do with the boat."

I watched attentively the old man's countenance, but failed to discover any emotion on his phlegmatic, sunburnt, weather-beaten face, over the features of which the flicker from the flames played merrily.

"If only we don't get into trouble." Michael began to give way.

"There will be no trouble if you don't let your tongue wag. If the Ataman should hear of it, we might get into a scrape, and they also. We have our work to do, and they have to be getting on. Is it far you have to go?" asked the old man again, though I had told him once before I was bound for Tiflis.

"That's a long way yet. The Ataman might detain them; then, when would they get to Tiflis? So let them be getting on their way. Eh?"

"Yes, let them go," all the shepherds agreed, as the old man, when he had finished speaking, closed his lips tightly, and cast an enquiring glance around him, as he fingered his grey beard.

"Well, my good fellows, be off, and God bless you!" he exclaimed with a gesture of dismissal. "We will see that the boat goes back, so don't trouble about that!"

"Many, many thanks, grandfather!" I said, taking off my cap.

"What are you thanking me for?"

"Thank you; thank you!" I repeated fervently.

"What are you thanking me for? That's

queer! I say, God bless you, and he thanks me! Were you afraid I'd send you to the devil, eh?"

"I'd done wrong and I was afraid," I answered.

"Oh!" And the old man lifted his eyebrows. "Why should I drive a man further along the wrong path? I'd do better by helping one along the way I'm going myself. Maybe, we shall meet again, and then we'll meet as friends. We ought to help one another where we can. Good-bye!"

He took off his large shaggy sheepskin cap, and bowed low to us. His comrades bowed too.

We enquired the way to Anapa, and started off. Shakro was laughing at something or other.

VIII.

"Why are you laughing?" I asked.

The old shepherd and his ethics of life had charmed and delighted me. I felt refreshed by the pure air of early morning, blowing straight into my face. I rejoiced, as I watched the sky gradually clearing, and felt that daylight was not far off. Before long the morning sun would rise in a clear sky, and we could look forward to a brilliantly fine day.

Shakro winked slyly at me, and burst out into a fresh fit of laughter. The hearty, buoyant ring in his laugh made me smile also. The few hours rest we had taken by the side of the shepherd's fire, and their excellent bread and bacon, had helped us to forget our exhausting voyage. Our bones still ached a little, but that would pass off with walking.

"Well, what are you laughing at? Are you glad that you are alive? Alive and not even hungry?"

Shakro shook his head, nudged me in the ribs, made a grimace, burst out laughing again, and at last said in his broken Russian: "You don't see what it is that makes me laugh? Well, I'll tell you in a minute. Do you know what I should have done if we had been taken before the Ataman? You don't know? I'd have told him that you had tried to drown me, and I should have begun to cry. Then they would have been sorry for me, and wouldn't have put me in prison! Do you see?"

At first I tried to make myself believe that it

was a joke ; but, alas ! he succeeded in convincing me he meant it seriously. So clearly and completely did he convince me of it, that, instead of being furious with him for such naïve cynicism, I was filled with deep pity for him, and incidentally for myself as well. What else but pity can one feel for a man who tells one in all sincerity, with the brightest of smiles, of his intention to murder one ? What is to be done with him if he looks upon such an action as a clever and delightful joke ?

I began to argue warmly with him, trying to show him all the immorality of his scheme. He retorted very candidly that I did not see where his interests lay, and had forgotten he had a false passport and might get into trouble in consequence. Suddenly a cruel thought flashed through my mind.

"Stay," said I, "do you really believe that I wanted to drown you ?"

"No ! When you were pushing me into the water I did think so ; but when you got in as well, then I didn't."

"Thank God !" I exclaimed. "Well, thanks for that, anyway !"

"Oh ! no, you needn't say thank you. I am

the one to say thank you. Were we not both cold when we were sitting round the fire? The overcoat was yours, but you didn't take it yourself. You dried it, and gave it to me. And took nothing for yourself. Thank you for that! You are a good fellow; I can see that. When we get to Tiflis, I will reward you. I shall take you to my father. I shall say to him: 'Here is a man whom you must feed and care for, while I deserve only to be kept in the stable with the mules.' You shall live with us, and be our gardener, and we will give you wine in plenty, and anything you like to eat. Ah! you will have a capital time! You will share my wine and food!"

He continued for some time, describing in detail the attractions of the new life he was going to arrange for me in his home in Tiflis.

And as he talked, I mused on the great unhappiness of men equipped with new morality and new aspirations—they tread the paths of life lonely and astray; and the fellow-travellers they meet on the way are aliens to them, unable to understand them. Life is a heavy burden for these lonely souls. Helplessly they drift hither and thither. They are like the good seed, wafted in the air, and dropping but rarely on to fruitful soil.

Daylight had broken. The sea far away shone with rosy gold.

"I am sleepy," said Shakro.

We halted. He lay down in a trench, which the fierce gusts of wind had dug out in the dry sand, near the shore. He wrapped himself, head and all, in the overcoat, and was soon sound asleep. I sat beside him, gazing dreamily over the sea.

It was living its vast life, full of mighty movement.

The flocks of waves broke noisily on the shore and rippled over the sand, that faintly hissed as it soaked up the water. The foremost waves, crested with white foam, flung themselves with a loud boom on the shore, and retreated, driven back to meet the waves that were pushing forwards to support them. Intermingling in the foam and spray, they rolled once more towards the shore, and beat upon it, struggling to enlarge the bounds of their realm. From the horizon to the shore, across the whole expanse of waters, these supple, mighty waves rose up, moving, ever moving, in a compact mass, bound together by the oneness of their aim. The sun shone more and more brightly on the crests of the breakers, which, in the distance on the horizon, looked blood-red. Not a drop went astray in the titanic heavings of the watery mass, impelled, it seemed, by some conscious aim, which it would soon attain by its vast rhythmic blows. Enchanting was the bold beauty of the foremost waves, as they dashed stubbornly upon the silent shore, and fine it was to see the whole sea, calm and united, the mighty sea, pressing on and ever on. The sea glittered now with all the colours of the rainbow, and seemed to take a proud, conscious delight in its own power and beauty.

A large steamer glided quietly round a point of land, cleaving the waters. Swaying majestically over the troubled sea, it dashed aside the threatening crests of the waves. At any other time this splendid, strong, flashing steamer would have set me thinking of the creative genius of man, who could thus enslave the elements. But now, beside me lay an untamed element in the shape of a man.

IX.

We were tramping now through the district of Terek. Shakro was indescribably ragged and dishevelled. He was surly as the devil, though he had plenty of food now, for it was easy to find work in these parts. He himself was not good at any kind of work. Once he got a small job on a thrashing-machine: his duty was to push aside the straw, as it left the machine; but after working half a day he left off, as the palms of his hands were blistered and sore. Another time he started off with me and some other workmen to root up trees, but he grazed his neck with a mattock.

We got on with our journey very slowly; we worked two days, and walked on the third day. Shakro ate all he could get hold of, and his gluttony prevented me from saving enough money to buy him new clothes. His ragged clothes were patched in the most fantastic way with pieces of various colours and sizes. I tried to persuade him to keep away from the beer-houses in the villages, and to give up drinking his favourite wines; but he paid no heed to my words.

With great difficulty I had, unknown to him, saved up five roubles, to buy him some new clothes. One day, when we were stopping in some village, he stole the money from my knapsack, and came in the evening, in a tipsy state, to the garden where I was working. He brought with him a fat country wench, who greeted me with the following words: "Good-day, you damned heretic!"

Astonished at this epithet, I asked her why she called me a heretic. She answered boldly: "Because you forbid a young man to love women, you devil. How can you forbid what is allowed by law? Damn you, you devil!"

Shakro stood beside her, nodding his head approvingly. He was very tipsy, and he rocked backwards and forwards unsteadily on his legs. His lower lip drooped helplessly. His dim eyes stared at me with vacant obstinacy.

"Come, what are you looking at us for? Give him his money!" shouted the undaunted woman.

"What money?" I exclaimed, astonished.

"Give it back at once; or I'll take you before the Ataman! Return the hundred and fifty roubles, which you borrowed from him in Odessa!"

What was I to do? The drunken creature

might really go and complain to the Ataman;—the Atamans were always very severe on any kind of tramp, and he might arrest us. Heaven only knew what trouble my arrest might inflict, not only on myself, but on Shakro! There was nothing for it but to try and outwit the woman, which was not, of course, a difficult matter. She was pacified after she had disposed of three bottles of vodka. She sank heavily to the ground, on a bed of melons, and fell asleep. Then I put Shakro to sleep also.

Early next morning we turned our backs on the village, leaving the woman sound asleep among the melons.

After his bout of drunkenness, Shakro, looking far from well, and with a swollen, blotchy face, walked slowly along, every now and then spitting on one side, and sighing deeply. I tried to begin a conversation with him, but he did not respond. He shook his unkempt head, as does a tired horse.

It was a hot day; the air was full of heavy vapours, rising from the damp soil, where the thick, lush grass grew abundantly—almost as high as our heads. Around us, on all sides, stretched a motionless sea of velvety green grass.

The hot air was steeped in strong sappy perfumes, which made one's head swim.

To shorten our way, we took a narrow path, where numbers of small red snakes glided about, coiling up under our feet. On the horizon, to our right, were ranges of cloudy summits flashing silvery in the sun. It was the mountain chain of the Daguestan Hills.

The stillness that reigned made one feel drowsy, and plunged one into a sort of dreamy state. Dark, heavy clouds, rolling up behind us, swept slowly across the heavens. They gathered at our backs, and the sky there grew dark, while in front of us it still showed clear, except for a few fleecy cloudlets, racing merrily across the open. But the gathering clouds grew darker and swifter. In the distance could be heard the rattle of thunder, and its angry rumbling came every moment nearer. Large drops of rain fell, pattering on the grass, with a sound like the clang of metal. There was no place where we could take shelter. It had grown dark. The patter of the rain on the grass was louder still, but it had a frightened, timid sound. There was a clap of thunder, and the clouds shuddered in a blue flash of lightning. Again it was dark, and the silvery chain of distant mountains was lost in the gloom. The rain now was falling in torrents, and one after another peals of thunder rumbled menacingly and incessantly over the vast steppe. The grass, beaten down by the wind and rain, lay flat on the ground, rustling faintly. Everything seemed quivering and troubled. Flashes of blinding lightning tore the storm-clouds asunder. The silvery, cold chain of the distant mountains sprang up in the blue flash and gleamed with blue light. When the lightning died away, the mountains vanished, as though flung back into an abyss of darkness. The air was filled with rumblings and vibrations, with sounds and echoes. The lowering, angry sky seemed purifying itself by fire, from the dust and the foulness which had risen towards it from the earth, and the earth, it seemed, was quaking in terror at its wrath. Shakro was shaking and whimpering like a scared dog. But I felt elated and lifted above commonplace life, as I watched the mighty, gloomy spectacle of the storm on the steppe. This unearthly chaos enchanted me and exalted me to an heroic mood, filling my soul with its wild, fierce harmony.

And I longed to take part in it, and to express, in some way or other, the rapture that filled my heart to overflowing, in the presence of the mysterious force which scatters gloom, and gathering clouds. The blue light which lit up the sky seemed to gleam in my soul too; and how was I to express my passion and my ecstasy at the grandeur of nature? I sang aloud, at the top of my voice. The thunder roared, the lightning flashed, the grass whispered, while I sang and felt myself in close kinship with nature's music. I was delirious, and it was pardonable, for it harmed no one but myself. I was filled with the desire to absorb, as much as possible, the mighty, living beauty and force that was raging on the steppe; and to get closer to it. A tempest at sea, and a thunderstorm on the steppes! I know nothing grander in nature. And so I shouted to my heart's content, in the absolute belief that I troubled no one, nor placed anyone in a position to criticise my action. But suddenly, I felt my legs seized, and I fell helplessly into a pool of water.

Shakro was looking into my face with serious and wrathful eyes.

"Are you mad? Aren't you? No? Well, then, be quiet! Don't shout! I'll cut your throat! Do you understand?"

I was amazed, and I asked him first what harm I was doing him?

"Why, you're frightening me! It's thundering; God is speaking, and you bawl. What are you thinking about?"

I replied that I had a right to sing whenever I chose. Just as he had.

"But I don't want to!" he said.

"Well, don't sing then!" I assented.

"And don't you sing!" insisted Shakro.

"Yes, I mean to sing!"

"Stop! What are you thinking about?" he went on angrily. "Who are you? You have neither home nor father, nor mother; you have no relations, no land! Who are you? Are you anybody, do you suppose? It's I am somebody in the world! I have everything!"

He slapped his chest vehemently.

"I'm a prince, and you—you're nobody—nothing! You say—you're this and that! Who else says so? All Koutais and Tiflis know me! You shall not contradict me! Do you hear? Are you not my servant? I'll pay ten times ever for all you have done for me. You *shall* obey me! You said yourself that God taught us to serve each other without seeking for a reward; but I'll reward you.

"Why will you annoy me, preaching to me, and frightening me? Do you want me to be like you? That's too bad! You can't make me like yourself! Foo! Foo!"

He talked, smacked his lips, snuffled, and sighed. I stood staring at him, open-mouthed with astonishment. He was evidently pouring out now all the discontent, displeasure and disgust, which had been gathering up during the whole of our journey. To convince me more thoroughly, he poked me in the chest from time to time with his forefinger, and shook me by the shoulder. During the most impressive parts of his speech he pushed up against me with his whole massive body. The rain was pouring down on us, the thunder never ceased its muttering, and to make me hear, Shakro shouted at the top of his voice. The tragic comedy of my position struck me more vividly than ever, and I burst into a wild fit of laughter. Shakro turned away and spat.

X

The nearer we draw to Tiflis, the gloomier and the surlier grew Shakro. His thinner, but still stolid face wore a new expression. Just before we reached Vladikavkas we passed through a Circassian village, where we obtained work in some maize fields.

The Circassians spoke very little Russian, and as they constantly laughed at us, and scolded us in their own language, we resolved to leave the village two days after our arrival; their increasing enmity had begun to alarm us.

We had left the village about ten miles behind, when Shakro produced from his shirt a roll of home-spun muslin, and handing it to me, exclaimed triumphantly:

"You need not work any more now. We can sell this, and buy all we want till we get to Tiflis! Do you see?"

I was moved to fury, and tearing the bundle from his hands, I flung it away, glancing back.

The Circassians are not to be trifled with! Only a short time before, the Cossacks had told us the following story.

A tramp, who had been working for some time

in a Circassian village, stole an iron spoon, and carried it away with him. The Circassians followed him, searched him, and found the iron spoon. They ripped open his body with a dagger, and after pushing the iron spoon into the wound, went off quietly, leaving him to his fate on the steppes. He was found by some Cossacks at the point of death. He told them this story, and died on the way to their village. The Cossacks had more than once warned us against the Circassians, relating many other edifying tales of the same sort. I had no reason to doubt the accuracy of these stories. I reminded Shakro of these facts. For some time he listened in silence to what I was saying; then, suddenly, showing his teeth and screwing up his eyes, he flew at me like a wild cat. We struggled for five minutes or so, till Shakro exclaimed angrily: "Enough! Enough!"

Exhausted with the struggle, we sat in silence for some time, facing each other. Shakro glanced covetously towards the spot, where I had flung the red muslin, and said:

"What were we fighting about? Fa—Fa—Fa! It's very stupid. I did not steal it from *you*, did, I? Why should you care? I was sorry for you that is why I took the linen. You have to work so hard, and I cannot help you in that way, so I thought I would help you by stealing. Tsè! Tsè!

I made an attempt to explain to him how wrong it was to steal.

"Hold your tongue, please! You're a blockhead!" he exclaimed, contemptuously; then added: "When one is dying of hunger, there is nothing for it but to steal; what sort of a life is this?"

I was silent, afraid of rousing his anger again. This was the second time he had committed a theft. Some time before, when we were tramping along the shores of the Black Sea, he stole a watch belonging to a fisherman. We had nearly come to blows then.

"Well, come along," he said; when, after a short rest, we had once more grown quiet and friendly.

So we trudged on. Each day made him grow more gloomy, and he looked at me strangely, from under his brows.

As we walked over the Darial Pass, he remarked: "Another day or two will bring us to Tiflis. Tsè! Tsè!"

He clicked his tongue, and his face beamed with delight.

"When I get home, they will ask me where I have been? I shall tell them I have been travelling. The first thing I shall do will be to take a nice bath. I shall eat a lot. Oh! what a lot. I have only to tell my mother 'I am hungry'! My father will forgive when I tell him how much trouble and sorrow I have undergone. Tramps are good sort of people! Whenever I meet a tramp, I shall always give him a rouble, and take him to the beer-house, and treat him to some wine. I shall tell him I was a tramp myself once. I shall tell my father all about you. I shall say: This man—he was like an elder brother to me. He lectured me, and beat me, the dog. He fed me, and now, I shall say, you must feed him. I shall tell him to feed you for a whole year. Do you hear that, Maxime?"

I liked to hear him talk in this strain; at those times he seemed so simple, so child-like. His words were all the more pleasant because I had not a single friend in all Tiflis. Winter was approaching. We had already been caught in a snowstorm in the Goudaour hills. I reckoned somewhat on Shakro's promises. We walked on rapidly till we reached Mesket, the ancient capital of Iberia. The next day we hoped to be in Tiflis.

I caught sight of the capital of the Caucasus in the distance, as it lay some five versts further on, nestling between two high hills. The end of our journey was fast approaching! I was rejoicing, but Shakro was indifferent. With a vacant look he fixed his eyes on the distance, and began spitting on one side; whilst he kept rubbing his stomach with a grimace of pain. The pain in his stomach was caused by his having eaten too many raw carrots, which he had pulled up by the wayside.

"Do you think I, a nobleman of Georgia, will show myself in my native town, torn and dirty as I am now? No, indeed, that I never could! We must wait outside till night. Let us rest here."

We twisted up a couple of cigarettes from our last bit of tobacco, and, shivering with cold, we sat down under the walls of a deserted building to have a smoke. The piercing cold wind seemed to cut through our bodies. Shakro sat humming a melancholy song; whilst I fell to picturing to myself a warm room, and other advantages of a settled life over a wandering existence.

"Let us move on now!" said Shakro, resolutely.

It had now become dark. The lights were twinkling down below in the town. It was a pretty sight to watch them flashing one after the other, out of the mist of the valley, where the town lay hidden.

"Look here, you give me your bashleek,* I want to cover my face up with it. My friends might recognise me."

I gave him my bashleek. We were already in Olga Street, and Shakro was whistling boldly.

"Maxime, do you see that bridge over yonder? The tram stops there. Go and wait for me there, please. I want first to go and ask a friend, who lives close by, about my father and mother."

"You won't be long, will you?"

"Only a minute. Not more!"

He plunged rapidly down the nearest dark narrow lane, and disappeared—disappeared for ever.

I never met him again—the man who was my

* A kind of hood worn by men to keep their ears warm.

fellow-traveller for nearly four long months; but I often think of him with a good-humoured feeling, and light-hearted laughter.

He taught me much that one does not find in the thick volumes of wise philosophers, for the wisdom of life is always deeper and wider than the wisdom of men.

ON A RAFT.

HEAVY clouds drift slowly across the sleepy river, and hang every moment lower and thicker. In the distance their ragged grey edges seem almost to touch the surface of the rapid and muddy waters, swollen by the floods of spring, and there, where they touch, an impenetrable wall rises to the skies, barring the flow of the river and the passage of the raft.

The stream, swirling against this wall—washing vainly against it with a wistful wailing swish—seems to be thrown back on itself, and then to hasten away on either side, where lies the moist fog of a dark spring night.

The raft floats onward and the distance opens out before it into heavy cloud—massed space. The banks of the rivers are invisible; darkness covers them, and the lapping waves of a spring flood seem to have washed them into space.

The river below has spread into a sea; whilst

the heavens above, swathed in cloud masses, hang heavy, humid, and leaden.*

There is no atmosphere, no colour in this grey blurred picture.

The raft glides down swiftly and noiselessly, whilst out of the darkness appears, suddenly bearing down on it, a steamer, pouring from its funnels a merry crowd of sparks, and churning up the water with the paddles of its great revolving wheels.

The two red forward lights gleam every moment larger and brighter, and the mast-head lantern sways slowly from side to side, as if winking mysteriously at the night. The distance is filled with the noise of the troubled water, and the heavy thud-thud of the engines.

* The river is the Volga, and the passage of strings of rafts down its stream in early spring is being described by the author. The allusion later on to the Brotherhood living in the Caucasus, refers to the persecuted Doukhobori, who have since been driven from their homes by the Russian authorities and have taken refuge in Canada.

In order to enter into the sociology of this story of Gorky's it must be explained that amongst ancient Russian folk-customs, as the young peasants were married at a very early age, the father of the bridegroom considered he had rights over his daughter-in-law. In later times, this custom, although occasionally continued, was held in disrepute amongst the peasantry; but that is has not entirely died out is proved by the little drama sketched in by the hand of a genius in "On a Raft."

"Look ahead!" is heard from the raft. The voice is that of a deep-chested man.

Two men are standing aft, grasping each a long pole, which propel the raft and act as rudders; Mitia, the son of the owner, a fair, weak, melancholy-looking lad of twenty-two; and Sergei, a peasant, hired to help in the work on board the raft, a bluff, healthy, red-bearded fellow, whose upper lip, raised with a mocking sneer, discloses a mouth filled with large, strong teeth.

"Starboard!" A second cry vibrates through the darkness ahead of the rafts.

"What are you shouting for; we know our business!" Sergei growls raspingly; pressing his expanded chest against the pole. "Ouch! Pull harder, Mitia!" Mitia pushes with his feet against the damp planks that form the raft, and with his thin hands draws towards him the heavy steering pole, coughing hoarsely the while.

"Harder, to starboard! You cursed loafers!" The master cries again, anger and anxiety in his voice.

"Shout away!" mutters Sergei. "Here's your miserable devil of a son, who couldn't break a straw across his knee, and you put him to steer a raft; and then you yell so that all the river hears you. You were mean enough not to take a second steersman; so now you may tear your throat to pieces shouting!"

These last words were growled out loud enough to be heard forward, and as if Sergei wished they should be heard.

The steamer passed rapidly alongside the raft sweeping the frothing water from under her paddle wheels. The planks tossed up and down in the wash, and the osier branches fastening them together, groaned and scraped with a moist plaintive sound.

The lit-up portholes of the steamer seem for a moment to rake the raft and the river with fiery eyes, reflected in the seething water, like luminous trembling spots. Then all disappears.

The wash of the steamer sweeps backwards and forwards, over the raft; the planks dance up and down. Mitia, swaying with the movements of the water, clutches convulsively the steering pole to save himself from falling.

"Well, well," says Sergei laughing. "So you're beginning to dance! Your father will start yelling again. Or he'll perhaps come and give you one or two in the ribs; then you'll dance to another tune! Port side now! Ouch!"

And with his muscles strung like steel springs, Sergei gives a powerful push to his pole, forcing it deep down into the water. Energetic, tall, mocking and rather malicious, he stands barefooted, rigid, as if a part of the planks; looking straight ahead, ready at any moment to change the direction of the raft.

"Just look there at your father kissing Marka! Aren't they a pair of devils? No shame, and no conscience. Why don't you get away from them, Mitia; away from these Pagan pigs? Why? Do you hear?"

"I hear," answered Mitia in a stifled voice, without looking towards the spot which Sergei pointed to through the darkness, where the form of Mitia's father could be seen.

"I hear," mocked Sergei, laughing ironically. "You poor half-baked creature! A pleasant state of things indeed!" he continued, encouraged by the apathy of Mitia. "And what a devil that old man is! He finds a wife for his son; he takes the son's wife away from him; and all's well! The old brute!"

Mitia is silent, and looks astern up the river,

where another wall of mist is formed. Now the clouds close in all round, and the raft hardly appears to move, but to be standing still in the thick dark water, crushed down by the heavy grey-black vapourous masses, which drift across the heavens, and bar the way.

The whole river seems like a fathomless, hidden whirlpool, surrounded by immense mountains, rising towards heaven, and capped with shrouding mists.

The stillness suffocates, and the water seems spell-bound with expectation, as it beats softly against the raft. A great sadness, and a timid questioning is heard in that faint sound;—the only voice of the night,—accentuating still more the silence. "We want a little wind now," says Sergei. "No it's not exactly wind we want—that would bring rain," he replies to himself, as be begins to fill his pipe. A match strikes, and the bubbling sound of a pipe being lighted is heard. A red gleam appears, throwing a glow over the big face of Sergei; and then, as the light dies down he is lost in the darkness.

"Mitia!" he cries. His voice is now less brutal and more mocking.

"What is it?" replies Mitia, without moving

his gaze from the distance, where he seems with his big sad eyes to be searching for something.

"How did it happen, mate?—How did it happen?"

"What?" answers Mitia, displeased.

"How did you come to marry? What a queer set out! How was it? You brought your wife home!—and then? Ha! ha! ha!"

"What are you cackling about? Look out there!" came threateningly across the river.

"Damned beast!" ejaculates with delight Sergei; and returns to the theme that interests him. "Come, Mitia; tell me; tell me at once—why not?"

"Leave me alone, Sergei," Mitia murmurs entreatingly; "I told you once."

But knowing by experience that Sergei will not leave him in peace, he begins hurriedly: "Well, I brought her home—and I told her: 'I can't be your husband, Marka; you are a strong girl, and I am a feeble, sick man. I didn't wish at all to marry you, but my father would force me to marry. He was always saying to me, 'Get married! get married!' I don't like women, I said: and you especially, you are too bold. Yes—and I can't have anything to do—with it.

Do you understand? For me, it disgusts me, and it is a sin. And children—one is answerable to God for one's children.'"

"Disgusts," yells Sergei, and laughs. "Well! and what did Marka reply? What?"

"She said, 'What shall I do now?' and then she began to cry. 'What have you got against me? Am I so dreadfully ugly?' She is shameless, Sergei, and wicked! 'With all this health and strength of mine, must I go to my father-in-law?' And I answered: 'If you like—go where you wish, but I can't act against my soul. If I had love for you, well and good; but being as it is, how is it possible? Father Ivan says it's the deadliest sin. We are not beasts, are we?' She went on crying: 'You have ruined my chances in life!' And I pitied her very much. 'It's nothing,' I said; 'things will come all right. Or,' I continued, 'you can go into a convent.' And she began to insult me. 'You are a stupid fool, Mitia!—a coward!'"

"Well, I'm blest!" exclaims Sergei, in a delighted whisper. "So you told her straight to go into a convent?"

"Yes, I told her to go," answers Mitia, simply.

"And she told you you were a fool?" queried Sergei, raising his voice.

"Yes, she insulted me."

"And she was right, my friend; yes, indeed, she was right! You deserve a proper hammering." And Sergei, changing suddenly his tone, continued with severity and authority: "Have you any right to go against the law? But you *did* go against it! Things are arranged in a certain way, and it's no use going against them! You mustn't even discuss them. But what did you do? You got some maggot into your head. A convent, indeed! Silly fool! What did the girl want? Did she want your convent? What a set of muddle-headed fools there seems to be now! Just think what's happened! *You*, you're neither fish nor fowl, nor good red-herring? And the girl's done for! She's living with an old man! And you drove the old man into sin! How many laws have *you* broken? You clever head!"

"Law, Sergei, is in the soul. There is one law for everyone. Don't do things that are against your soul, and you will do no evil on the earth," answered Mitia, in a slow, conciliatory tone, and nodding his head.

"But you did do evil," answered Sergei, energetically. "In the soul! A fine idea! There are many things in the soul. Certain things *must* be forbidden. The soul, the soul! You must first understand it, my friend, and then——"

"No, it's not so, Sergei," replied Mitia with warmth, and he seemed to be inspired. "The soul, my friend, is always as clear as dew. It's true, its voice lies deep down within us, and is difficult to hear; but if we listen, we can never be mistaken. If we act according to what is in our soul, we shall always act according to the will of God. God is in the soul, and, therefore, the law must be in it. The soul was created by God, and breathed by God into man. We have only to learn to look into it—and we must look into it without sparing our own feelings."

"You sleepy devils! look ahead there!" The voice thundered from the forward part of the raft, and swept back down the river. In the strength of the sound one could recognise that the owner of the voice was healthy, energetic, and pleased with himself. A man with large and conscious vitality. He shouted, not because he had to give a necessary order to the steersmen, but because his soul was full of life and strength, and this life and strength wanted to find free expression, so it rushed forth in that thunderous and forceful sound.

"Listen to the old blackguard shouting," continued Sergei with delight, looking ahead with a piercing glance, and smiling. "Look at them billing and cooing like a pair of doves! Don't you ever envy them, Mitia?"

Mitia watched with indifference the working of the two forward oars, held by two figures who moved backwards and forwards, forming sometimes as they touched each other one compact and dark mass.

"So you say you don't envy them?" repeated Sergei.

"What is it to me? It's their sin, and they must answer for it," replied Mitia, quietly.

"Hm!" ironically interjected Sergei, whilst he filled his pipe.

Once more the small red patch of light glowed in the darkness; and the night grew thicker, and the grey clouds sank lower towards the swollen river.

"Where did you get hold of all that fine stuff, or does it come to you naturally? But you don't take after your father, my lad! Your father's a fine old chap. Look at him! he's fifty-two now, and see what a strapping wench he's carrying on with! She's as fine a woman as ever wore shoe-leather. And she loves him; it's no use denying it! She loves him, my lad! One can't help admiring him, he's such a trump, your father—he's the king of trumps! When he's at work, it's worth while watching him. And then, he's rich! And then, look how he's respected! And his head's screwed on the right way. Yes. And you? You're not a bit like either your father or your mother? What would your father have done, Mitia, do you think, if old Anfesa had lived? That would have been a good joke! I should have liked to have seen how she'd have settled him! She was the right sort of woman, your mother! a real plucky one, she was! They were well matched!

Mitia remained silent, leaning on the pole, and staring at the water.

Sergei ceased talking. Forward on the raft was heard a woman's shrill laugh, followed by the deeper laugh of a man. Their figures, blurred by the mist, were nearly invisible to Sergei, who, however, watched them curiously. The man appeared as a tall figure, standing with legs wide apart, holding a pole, and half turned towards a shorter woman's figure, leaning on another pole, and standing a few paces away. She shook her forefinger at the man, and giggled provokingly.

Sergei turned away his head with a sigh, and after a few moments' silence began to speak again.

"Confound it all, but how jolly they seem together; it's good to see! Why can't I have something like that? I, a waif and a stray! I'd never leave such a woman! I'd always have my arms round her, and there'd be no mistake about *my* loving the little devil! I've never had any luck with women! They don't like ginger hair—women don't. No. She's a woman with fancies, she is! She's a sly little devil! She wants to see life! Are you asleep, Mitia?"

"No," answered Mitia, quietly.

"Well, how are you going to live? To tell the truth, you're as solitary as a post! That seems pretty hard! Where can you go? You can't earn your living among strangers. You're too absurd! What's the use of a man who can't stand up for himself? A man's got to have teeth and claws in this world! They'll all have a go at you. Can you stick up for yourself? How would you set about it? Damn it all; where the devil *could* you go?"

"I," said Mitia, suddenly arousing herself; "I shall go away. I shall go in the autumn to the Caucasian Mountains, and that will be the end of it all. My God! If only I could get away from you all! Soulless, godless men! To get away from you, that's my only hope! What do you live for? Where is your God? He's nothing but a name! Do you live in Christ? You are wolves; that's what you are! But over there live other men, whose souls live in Christ. Their hearts contain love, and they are athirst for the salvation of the world. But you—you are beasts, spewing out filth. But other men there are; I have seen them; they called me, and I must go to them. They gave me the book of Holy Writ, and they said: 'Read, man of God, our beloved brother, read the word of truth!' And I read, and my soul was renewed by the word of God. I shall go away. I shall leave all you ravening wolves. You are rending each other's flesh! Accursed be ye!"

Mitia spoke in a passionate whisper, as if

overpowered by the intensity of his contemplative rapture, his anger with the ravening wolves, and his desire to be with those other men, whose souls aspired towards the salvation of the world. Sergei was taken aback. He remained quiet for some time, open-mouthed, holding his pipe in his hand. After a few moments' thought he glanced round, and said in a deep, rough voice: "Damn it all! Why you're turned a bad 'un all at once! Why did you read that book? It was very likely an evil one. Well, be off, be off! If not, there'll be an end of you! Be off with you before you become a regular beast yourself! And who are these fellows in the Caucasus? Monks? Or what?"

But the fire of Mitia's spirit died down as quickly as it had been kindled to a flame; he gasped with the exertion as he worked the pole, and muttered to himself below his breath.

Sergei waited some time for the answer which did not come. His simple hardy nature was quelled by the grim and death-like stillness of the night. He wanted to recall the fullness of life, to wake the solitude with sound, to disturb and trouble the hidden meditative silence of the leaden mass of water, flowing slowly to the sea;

and of the dull threatening clouds hanging motionless in the air. At the other end of the raft there was life, and it called on him to live.

Forward, he could hear every now and then bursts of contented laughter, exclamations, sounds that seemed to stand out against the silence of this night, laden with the breath of spring, and provoking such passionate life desires.

"Hold hard, Mitia! you'll catch it again from the old man! Look out there!" said Sergei, who could not stand the silence any longer; and watching Mitia, who aimlessly moved his pole backwards and forwards in the water.

Mitia, wiping his moist brow, stood quietly leaning with his breast against the pole, and panting.

"There are few steamers to-night;" continued Sergei; "We've only passed one these many hours." Seeing that Mitia had no intention of answering, Sergei replied quietly to himself: "It's because its too early in the season. It's only just beginning. We shall soon be at Kazan. The Volga pulls hard. She has a mighty strong back, that can carry all. Why are you standing still like that? Are you angry? Hi, there, Mitia!"

"What's the matter?" Mitia cried in a vexed tone.

"Nothing, you strange fellow; but why can't you talk? You are always thinking. Leave it alone! Thinking is bad for a man. A wise sort of fellow you are! You think and think, and all the time you can't understand that you're a fool at bottom. Ha! Ha!" And Sergei, satisfied with his superiority, cleared his throat, remained quiet for a moment, whistled a note, and then continued to develop his theme.

"Thinking? Is that an occupation for a working man? Look at your father; he doesn't think much; he lives. He loves your wife, and they laugh at you together; you wise fool! That's about it! Just listen to them! Blast them! I believe Marka's already with child. Never fear, the child won't feature you. He'll be a fine, lusty lad, like Silan himself! But he'll be *your* child! Ha! Ha! Ha! He'll call *you* father! And you wont be his father, but his brother; and his real father will be his grandfather! That's a nice state of things!

What a filthy family! But they're a strapping pair! Isn't that true, Mitia?"

"Sergei!" In a passionate, sobbing whisper. "In the name of Christ I entreat you don't tear my soul to pieces, don't brand me with fire. Leave me alone. Do be quiet! In the name of God and of Christ, I beg you not to speak to me! Don't disturb me! Don't drain my heart's blood! I'll throw myself in the river, and yours will be the sin, and a great sin it will be! I should lose my soul; don't force me to it! For God's sake, I entreat you!"

The silence of the night was troubled with shrill, unnatural sobbing; and Mitia fell on the deck of the raft, as if a blast from the overhanging clouds had struck him down.

"Come, come!" growled Sergei, anxiously watching his mate writhing on the deck, as if scorched with fire. "What a strange man! He ought to have told me if it was not—if it was not quite——"

"You've been torturing me all the way? Why? Am I your enemy?" Mitia sobbed again.

"You're a strange lad! a rum 'un!" murmured Sergei, confused and offended. "How could *I* know? I couldn't tell you'd take on like that!"

"Understand, then, that I want to forget! To forget for ever! My shame, my terrible torture. You're a cruel lot! I shall go away, and stay away for ever! I can't stand it any more!"

"Yes, be off with you!" cried Sergei across the raft, accentuating his exclamation with a loud and cynical curse. Then he seemed to shrink together, as if himself afraid of the terrible drama which was unfolding itself before him; drama, which he was now compelled to understand. . . . .

"Hullo! there! I'm calling you! are you deaf!" sounded up the river the voice of Silan. "What are you about there? What are you bawling about? Ahoy! Ahoy!"

It seemed as if Silan enjoyed shouting, and breaking the heavy silence of the river with his deep voice, full of strength and health. The cries succeeded each other, thrilling the warm, moist air, and seeming to crush down on Mitia's feeble form. He rose, and once more pressed his body against the steering pole. Sergei shouted in reply to the master with all his strength, and cursed him at the same time under his breath.

The two voices broke through and filled the silence of the night. Then they seemed to meet in one deep note like the sound of a great horn. Once more rising to shrillness, they floated in the air, gradually sank away—and were lost.

Silence reigned once more.

Through the cleft clouds, on the dark water the yellow splashes of moonlight fell, and after glittering a moment disappeared, swept away in the moist gloom.

The raft continued on its way down stream amidst silence and darkness.

II.

Near one of the forward poles stood Silan Petroff in a red shirt, open at the neck, showing his powerful throat and hairy chest, hard as an anvil. A thatch of grey hair fell over his forehead, under which laughed great black warm eyes. His sleeves, turned up to the elbow, showed the veins standing out on his arms as they held the pole. Silan was leaning slightly forward, and looking watchfully ahead. Marka stood a few paces from him, glancing with a satisfied smile at the strong form of her lover. They were both silent and busy with their several thoughts. He was peering into the distance, and she followed the movements of his virile, bearded face.

"That must be a fisherman's fire," said he, turning towards her.

"It's all right; we're keeping on our course, Ouch!" And he puffed out a full, hot breath, and gave a powerful shove with his pole.

"Don't tire yourself, Mashourka," he continued, watching her, as with her pole she made a skilful movement.

She was round and plump, with black bright eyes and ruddy cheeks; barefooted, dressed only in a damp petticoat, which clung to her body, and showed the outline of her figure. She turned her face to Silan and, smiling pleasantly, said: "You take too much care of me; I'm all right!"

"I kiss you, but I don't take care of you," answered Silan, moving his shoulders.

"That's not good enough!" she replied, provokingly; and they both were silent, looking at each other with desiring eyes.

Under the rafts, the water gurgled musically. On the right bank, very far off, a cock crew. Swaying lightly under their feet, the raft floated on towards a point where the darkness dissolved into lighter tones, and the clouds took on themselves clearer shapes and less sombre hues.

"Silan Pertovitch, do you know what they were shouting about there? I know. I bet you I know. It was Mitia who was complaining about us to Sergei; and it was he who cried out with trouble, and Sergei was cursing us!"

Marka questioned anxiously Silan's face, which, after her words, became grim and coldly stubborn.

"Well!" shortly.

"Well, that's all!"

"If that's all, there was nothing to say."

"Don't get angry."

"Angry with you? I should like to be angry with you, but I can't."

"You love Marsha?" she whispered, coaxingly leaning towards him.

"You bet!" answered Silan, with emphasis, stretching out towards her his powerful arms. "Come now, don't tease me!"

She twisted her body with the movements of a cat, and once more leaned towards him.

"We shall upset the steering again," whispered he, kissing her face which burnt under his lips.

"Shut up now! They can see us at the other end;" and motioning aft with her head, she struggled to free herself, but he held her more tightly still with one arm, and managed the pole with the other hand.

"They can see us? let them see us. I spit on them all! I'm sinning, that's true; I know it; and shall have to answer for it to God; but still you never were his wife; you were free; you belonged to yourself. He's suffering, I know. And what about me? Is my position a pleasant one? It is true that you were not his wife; but all the same; with my position, how must I feel now? Is it not a dreadful sin before God? It is a sin! I know it all, and I've gone through everything! Because it's a thing worth doing! We love only once, and we may die any day. Oh! Marka! If I'd only waited a month before marrying you to Mitia, nothing of this would have happened. Directly after the death of Anfisa I would have sent my friends to propose for you, and all would have been right! Right before the law; without sin, without shame. That was my mistake, and this mistake will take away from me five or ten years of my life. Such a mistake as that makes an old man of one before one's time."

Silan Petroff spoke with decision, but quietly, whilst an expression of inflexible determination flashed from his face, giving him the appearance of a man who was ready then and there to fight and struggle for the right to love.

"Well, it's all right now; don't trouble yourself any more. We have talked about it more than once already," whispered Marka, freeing herself gently from his arms, and returning to her oar.

He began working his pole backwards and forwards rapidly and energetically, as if he wished to get rid of the load that weighed on his breast, and cast a shadow over his fine face.

Day broke gradually.

The clouds, losing their density, crept slowly away on every side, as if reluctantly giving place to the sunlight. The surface of the river grew lighter, and took on it the cold gleam of polished steel.

"Not long ago he talked with me about it. 'Father, he said, is it not a deadly shame for you, and for me? Give her up!' He meant *you;* explained Silan, and smiled. 'Give her up,' he said; 'return to the right path!' 'My dear son,' I said, 'go away if you want to save your skin! I shall tear you to pieces like a rotten rag! There will be nothing left of your great virtue! It's a sorrow to me to think that I'm your father! You puny wretch!' He trembled. 'Father,' he said, 'am I in the wrong?' 'You are,' I said, 'you whining cur! because you are in my way! You are,' I said, 'because you can't stand up for yourself! You lifeless, rotten carrion! If only,' I said, 'you were strong, one could kill you; but even that isn't possible! One pities you, poor, wretched creature!' He only wept. Oh, Marka! This sort of thing makes one good for nothing. Any one else would—would get their heads out of this noose as soon as possible, but we are in it, and we shall perhaps tighten it round each other's necks!"

"What do you mean?" said Marka, looking at him fearfully, as he stood there grim, strong and cold.

CPSIA information can be obtained at www.ICGtesting.com
Printed in the USA
BVOW08s1424050315

390501BV00020B/176/P